MW01093907

The Hymns of Easter

Daily Lent and Easter Devotions
on Classic Hymns

Alan Vermilye

BROWN CHAIR BOOKS
BOOKS THAT INSPIRE

The Hymns of Easter
Daily Lent and Easter Devotions on Classic Hymns

ISBN-13 Paperback: 978-1-948481-48-9

ISBN-13 Hardback: 978-1-948481-50-2

To learn more about this book or to order additional copies, visit
www.BrownChairBooks.com.

Version 1

Contents

Introduction

S everal years ago, I released *The Carols of Christmas, Volume 1* with absolutely no idea how it would be received. To my surprise, it rocketed to the top of Amazon's bestseller list and became one of the most popular Christmas devotionals that season. I completed the series over the next couple of years with volumes two and three, with both books performing exceptionally well. I love hearing from so many readers who enjoy these devotional books and are discovering the history behind these carols that help make the Christmas season special.

Given the devotional's popularity for Advent, I wondered how well a Lent/Easter devotional featuring traditional Easter hymns would be received. For those unfamiliar with Lent, or those whose churches don't observe it, you might be wondering what it's all about and if it's for you. In short, Lent is a time traditionally set aside for Christians to fast, pray, and prepare their hearts to celebrate the resurrection of Jesus Christ.

Although modern denominations observe the practice in diverse ways, Lent is an ancient discipline that dates back more than 1,700 years. It remained unchanged for centuries until the emergence of new ideas during the Protestant Reformation, when the long-held traditions began to fade, eventually disappearing from the mainline church. However, in more recent years, Christians of all denominations have rediscovered the value of observing Lent, using it for spiritual reflection and preparation for Easter.

Lent begins each spring and is observed for forty days, excluding Sundays, which are set aside for celebrating the resurrection. Why forty days? There is a significant biblical connection to the number forty. For forty days, a flood engulfed the earth during Noah's time, purging it of evil. Moses received the Ten Commandments after forty days on Mt. Sinai, and the Hebrews wandered in the wilderness for forty years before entering their Promised Land. And before starting his ministry, Jesus spent forty days and nights in the desert praying and fasting. Tradition even holds that Jesus remained in the tomb for forty hours before his Easter resurrection. Early Christians used these facts to justify a forty-day period of spiritual preparation and cleansing before Easter.

I sincerely hope these next forty days will be a season of reflection and prayer preparing your heart to celebrate the risen Savior. But also, I pray the spiritual disciplines you develop over the next forty days become ingrained and a constant reminder of what we should be doing all year.

God bless,
Alan

How to Use This Devotional

For those of you familiar with *The Carols of Christmas* format, you will find *The Hymns of Easter* format slightly different. Rather than twenty-eight consecutive days over the four weeks of Advent, Lent last forty nonconsecutive days, beginning on Ash Wednesday and ending on the Saturday before Easter, excluding Sundays. *(Although I know some denominations are different, so you can adjust as needed.)*

You'll find the first week of the devotional to be short, beginning on Ash Wednesday to Saturday. Each of the next six weeks begins on Monday, where you will read about the hymn's history followed by four days of devotions. Saturdays are for review and reflection on the week's hymn and getting caught up. While Sundays do hold significant meaning during the Lenten season, they are excluded from the forty-day count, serving as a time for rest and reflection on the risen Savior.

The devotional is designed to be used during the forty days of Lent, but its flexible format allows you to use it in a way that works best for you. For the daily schedule and hymn list, please refer to the table of contents.

Small Group Discussion Questions

For those that would like to read the devotional in community with a small group, I've created a free study guide, available at www.BrownChairBooks.com/free-resources-sign-up.

Wednesday, Day 1

"HALLELUJAH CHORUS"—A HISTORY

I know what you're thinking: "Wait a second! Isn't this hymn traditionally sung during Christmas?" The answer falls somewhere in between yes and no. The truth is, Christmas is often synonymous with the timeless tradition of attending or being part of a performance of Handel's *Messiah*, featuring the iconic "Hallelujah Chorus." However, when you consider the 280-year history of this hymn, this is a relatively recent development. Ironically, George Frideric Handel, one of the most famous composers of his time, initially composed *Messiah* as an Easter offering, with a larger portion of the text focusing on Christ's death and resurrection than his birth. Furthermore, the inaugural performance of this magnificent masterpiece took place during Passion Week in 1742 and remained a cherished tradition for over one hundred fifty years. So how did this beloved oratorio, originally tied to Easter, find its way into the repertoire of Christmas performances?

The fascinating story begins in the small town of Halle, Germany, where, on February 24, 1685, George Frideric Handel was born. His parents had high expectations for him as he grew up. His mother, the daughter of a Lutheran preacher, instilled in him a strong spiritual foundation, while his father, a surgeon, had his sights set on his son pursuing a career in law. Young George, on the other hand, had a deep passion for music, and even at a young age, his remarkable talent was evident. His mother, determined to support her son's musical talents, bought a harpsichord that they kept hidden in the attic, away from his disapproving father.

Despite his initial resistance, even his father couldn't ignore his son's talent and eventually consented to his training with Frideric Wilhelm Zachow, a respected local composer and organist. Handel's only formal music instruction came at this time. By the age of twelve, he had already composed his first musical composition, and by nineteen, he had mastered most orchestral instruments.

Even though Handel's father passed away when he was only twelve, plans were already in place for his education in law. Handel, torn between his passion for music and his father's expectations, reluctantly enrolled in law studies at the University of Halle. However, his time as a student didn't last long. At the age of eighteen, in 1703, he made the decision to fully dedicate himself to music.

He traveled to Hamburg, where he accepted a violinist's position at an opera house and, in his free time, supplemented his income by teaching private music lessons. Here, Handel found his inspiration to compose operas, and his first one, *Almira*, marked the beginning of his illustrious career in early 1705. His debut opera captivated audiences from the very first note, leading to an impressive twenty-performance run. In 1706 he made the transition to Italy and continued his string of successful operas, including *Rodrigo* and *Agrippina*.

Leaving Italy in 1710, Handel ventured to London. His destination held an exciting opportunity: a commission from the King's Theatre to create an opera. Unsurprisingly, Handel rose to the challenge and, in an astonishing display of talent and speed, composed *Rinaldo* in just two weeks. Handel's success opened the doors to a new chapter in his career, as he found himself composing and performing for esteemed English royalty, such as Queen Anne and King George I.

Then, in 1719, Handel eagerly accepted the invitation to become the orchestra master for the Royal Academy of Music, the first Italian opera company in London. Over the years, he created numerous operas with the academy, each one a masterpiece of music and storytelling, yet they failed to bring the struggling academy the financial success it desperately needed.

Following some internal conflict at the academy, Handel made the bold decision to establish his own company in 1727, which he named the New Royal Academy of Music. Now at the helm of his own company, Handel diligently produced two Italian operas a year for the next decade, despite the declining ticket sales and popularity of the format in London.

By the spring of 1741, Handel was heavily in debt following a string of musical failures and was facing bankruptcy and the threat of debtors' prison. As his opera productions grew more elaborate, expenses climbed, including hiring musicians and singers only from Italy. Also, some Church of England authorities were apparently critical of him and his work. On top of everything else, his health began to fail as he struggled with failing eyesight and paralysis on his right side from a recent stroke. The weight of his crumbling career and uncertain future plunged him into a deep depression. On April 8, 1741, Handel gave what he believed to be his final concert. Just when he thought all hope was gone, two key events happened that would forever alter his career and leave an indelible mark on music history.

Charles Jennens, Jr., a wealthy admirer of Handel's music and a literary scholar, had selected Old and New Testament scriptures documenting the prophecies about the Messiah—specifically related to his birth, death on the cross, and resurrection. He carefully arranged the words into a text, envisioning a magnificent choral composition that Handel would bring to life, and sent it to him. In a letter to a friend, Jennens expressed his desire to convince Handel to compose music for his text on the life of the Messiah and present it during Passion Week the following year. He was convinced that if Handel did it, it would be his best composition to date.

Then a group of charitable organizations in Dublin, Ireland, provided financial backing for Handel to compose a new piece for a benefit performance dedicated to the cause of freeing men from debtors' prison. Handel would also be paid a commission for composing the piece, providing him with the means to overcome his own financial challenges. Contemplating the generous offer, Handel's hand instinctively reached for Jennens's text, and a wave of inspiration washed over him. He then immersed himself into writing what's now become the world's most widely performed oratorio, *Messiah*.

What's truly remarkable is the story behind the writing of this renowned piece that centers on the life of Christ. In a burst of creativity, Handel wrote the three-hour work in a mere twenty-four days! It's said that Handel would literally write from morning to night, never leaving his house during those three weeks, not sleeping, and barely eating. When his assistants brought him his meals, they were often left uneaten. According to the music commentator Miles Hoffman, Handel would have had to write fifteen notes per minute for over three weeks, working ten hours a day, to create *Messiah*.

Although Handel said the music came to him in rapid succession, he ultimately credited the completion of this work to one thing: joy. He stated that while writing feverishly, the music came to him, driven by an unseen composer. He described feeling immense joy as the words and music filled his heart and mind.

One day during this time, his assistant made repeated calls outside the composer's room but received no response. Sensing something was not right, he entered the room to find Handel weeping and proclaiming, "I have seen the face of God." In his hands, he held the famous conclusion to his masterpiece, "Hallelujah Chorus."

After completing his masterpiece, Handel faced the challenge of deciding where to premiere it. His own waning popularity in London and the lukewarm reception of his recent works concerned him, and he could not risk another failure. Hoping for a fresh start for his work and career, he decided to present *Messiah* in Dublin the following year. He carefully organized a string of concerts at a music hall, starting in February 1742, that led up to the grand premiere of *Messiah* in April during Passion Week. The concert served both as a charitable benefit concert and an Easter tribute.

His plan worked! Premiere tickets were in such high demand that advertisements urged ladies to forego their hoop skirts and gentlemen to forgo their swords, ensuring a more spacious concert hall. According to one source, the proceeds from the event helped free 142 men from debtors' prison. Despite receiving rave reviews in Dublin, the performances of *Messiah* didn't fare as well in London the following season.

In London, Handel made the unfortunate decision to secure a large performing venue that also had a notorious reputation. Many considered it an unconventional and even sacrilegious choice for presenting the sacred story of the Messiah. Unable to overcome what became a marketing disaster, performances were canceled and eventually scrapped altogether. *Messiah*, sadly, seemed destined to be forgotten like some of Handel's other compositions, until an unexpected savior emerged.

The Foundling Hospital was London's first orphanage to take in abandoned children. The charity's founders believed that for it to be successful, it had to establish a strong presence in the public's mind. So artists and sculptors were invited to contribute their works for display in the new building, thus establishing the first public art gallery. Once there, fashionable society would witness the best in contemporary art and music as well as the heartwarming sight of children enjoying their mealtime and singing in the chapel, all in support of a truly deserving cause.

In May 1749 Handel, a known philanthropist, approached the hospital's governors and offered to conduct a benefit concert. The program featured a composition he had written specifically for the charity, as well as some of his other works, and concluded with "Hallelujah Chorus," a piece that was unfamiliar to most of the audience. The benefit concert was a huge musical and financial success and left such an impression that Handel was eagerly invited back the next year, where he captivated the audience with a breathtaking performance of the entire *Messiah* oratorio. Performances of *Messiah* became an Easter-time tradition for the Foundling Hospital, raising over a million dollars in today's money. It was a vital source of income that allowed the hospital to continue to provide a home for vulnerable, abandoned children. Many years after Handel's death, one scholar wrote, "*Messiah* has fed the hungry, clothed the naked, fostered the orphan...more than any other single musical production in this or any country."

Suddenly *Messiah*'s popularity soared to new heights, with performances springing up all across England during Passion Week, a time when opera performances were banned. However, *Messiah* was an oratorio, and theater owners believed it would undoubtedly attract a large audience given its focus on the birth, death, and resurrection of Jesus. Their controversial decision to offer the performance led to it reaching an even wider audience. Whether in small English towns or big cities, large numbers of people eagerly attended the annual presentation of Handel's work, and it would remain that way for over one hundred fifteen years.

The dawn of the 1900s brought a realization among charities that Christmas, with its longer season and the inherent generosity of people, offered a more favorable environment for fundraising. This led to *Messiah* becoming an essential part of both Christmas and Easter celebrations in England. Only in the 1960s did *Messiah* experience a notable shift, becoming primarily associated with Christmas—a tradition that spread throughout the United States and, eventually, the world. Across the globe, countless performances of *Messiah* by professional and amateur ensembles take place every December.

The "Hallelujah Chorus" even developed its own tradition over time. According to legend, King George II of England was so moved by the "Hallelujah Chorus" at a *Messiah* performance at a London premier that he rose to his feet. Everyone else followed his example, and the tradition has carried on to this day.

Whether performed during Easter or Christmas, *Messiah*, with its powerful "Hallelujah Chorus," has unquestionably been used as a means to evangelize and spread the gospel to a wide audience. Moreover, the message of *Messiah* has served as a source of inspiration for millions of people, compelling them to donate to those in need, all in the name of Christ.

Most composers from that era never expected their music would endure beyond their lifetime. Handel's *Messiah* is certainly the outlier, being perhaps the oldest continuously performed composition from any composer. Yet George Frideric Handel refused to take the credit. In a beautiful gesture, at the end of *Messiah*, Handel paid homage to his faith by including the letters "SDG" for Soli Deo Gloria, which means "To God Alone the Glory."

"Hallelujah! Chorus" Lyrics

Hallelujah!, Hallelujah!, Hallelujah!, Hallelujah!, Hallelujah!.
Hallelujah!, Hallelujah!, Hallelujah!, Hallelujah!, Hallelujah!.

For the Lord God omnipotent reigneth.
Hallelujah!, Hallelujah!, Hallelujah!, Hallelujah!.
For the Lord God omnipotent reigneth.
Hallelujah!, Hallelujah!, Hallelujah!, Hallelujah!.
For (Hallelujah!) the Lord (Hallelujah!) God omnipotent reign-(Hallelujah!)-eth.
Hallelujah!, Hallelujah!, Hallelujah!, Hallelujah!, Hallelujah!.

The kingdom of this world is become.
The kingdom of our lord and of his Christ, and of his Christ.
And he shall reign for ever and ever.
For ever and ever Hallelujah! Hallelujah!

King of Kings. For ever and ever
Hallelujah! Hallelujah!.
And lord of lords. For ever and ever
Hallelujah! Hallelujah!.
King of Kings. For ever and ever
Hallelujah! Hallelujah!.
And lord of lords. For ever and ever
Hallelujah! Hallelujah!.
King of Kings. For ever and ever
Hallelujah! Hallelujah!.
And lord of lords. For ever and ever
Hallelujah! Hallelujah!.
King of kings and lord of lords.

And he shall reign for ever for ever and ever.
King of kings, and lord of lords. King of kings and lord of lords.
And he shall reign for ever for ever and ever.

For ever and ever. For ever and ever.
Hallelujah! Hallelujah! Hallelujah! Hallelujah!

Thursday, Day 2
FOR THE LORD GOD OMNIPOTENT REIGNETH

And I heard, as it were, the voice of a great multitude, as the sound of many waters, and as the sound of mighty thunderings, saying, "Alleluia! For the Lord God Omnipotent reigns! Revelation 19:6 NKJV

Have you ever planned a wedding? If so, you know that as the date approaches, anticipation and emotions steadily build. I would even go as far as to say that my wife and I are experts in this field, having successfully married off three daughters in under two years. What I can absolutely attest to is that you spend countless months meticulously planning for one extraordinary day, painstakingly attending to even the smallest of details. Then, when that long-awaited day finally arrives and everything goes off without a hitch, you can't help but feel an overwhelming urge to shout, "Hallelujah!" from the depths of your soul.

The book of Revelation evokes a similar sense throughout as it gradually builds up to chapter nineteen, where a glorious celebration is to take place. In previous chapters, God clearly demonstrates his power and authority as he pours out his wrath on the anti-Christian world system, destroying it forever. Suddenly, in chapter nineteen, the Apostle John's vision shifts from the earthly realm to the heavenly realm, where he stands witness to the long-awaited wedding of the Lamb. While the sight was undoubtedly amazing, he could never have anticipated the magnificent symphony of sounds that awaited him.

What's interesting is that the word "hallelujah" is found only four times in the New Testament, all within the first six verses of Revelation nineteen. I imagine the first three being a crescendo of hallelujahs, with each time growing more intense. Then, in a breathtaking moment, the groom takes his bride, and the mighty multitude of heaven raises their voices in unison, proclaiming one final hallelujah! The sound had to be deafening as shouts of praise and glory boomed throughout heaven. There is no sound on Earth that could possibly compare to what John experienced—the ultimate hallelujah chorus!

The more effort poured into wedding planning, the higher the likelihood of a flawless celebration. Though no amount of planning can entirely eliminate all risks or unexpected hiccups. But with God, it's different. We can have complete confidence that our all-powerful King will carry out his wedding plans flawlessly and on schedule.

This takes on even greater importance when we consider the death, burial, and resurrection of Jesus Christ. By placing our belief in Jesus as the one who paid the price for our sins, was buried, and triumphed over sin and death by rising from the dead after three days, we will be among the mighty multitude that will joyfully sing the hallelujah chorus on that wonderful wedding day.

Friday, Day 3

AND HE SHALL REIGN FOR EVER AND EVER

Then the seventh angel sounded: And there were loud voices in heaven, saying, "The kingdoms of this world have become the kingdoms of our Lord and of His Christ, and He shall reign forever and ever!" Revelation 11:15 NKJV

The unexpected death of his brother, Emperor Titus, in the summer of AD 81 paved the way for Domitian's rise to power. As he took the reins of the Roman empire, Domitian quickly turned into a despotic ruler notorious for his impulsive and irresponsible decisions, particularly his enforcement of a practice called "emperor worship."

While it was not an unusual practice for emperors to be deified after their deaths, what set Domitian apart was his desire to be worshipped while still alive. He proclaimed himself "Lord and God" and went to great lengths, erecting statues and building temples dedicated to himself in cities across the empire, including the biblical city of Ephesus. Citizens lived in constant fear as they were forced to worship and offer sacrifices to Domitian under the threat of brutal public executions for any that defied him.

It was during this time that the Ephesus church was under the leadership of none other than the last remaining apostle, John. Now well into his nineties, John fearlessly stood against Domitian's ruthless enforcement tactics, and his defiance eventually caught the attention of the self-aggrandizing emperor. As a result, the elderly apostle was exiled to the island of Patmos in AD 94. This rocky and desolate location, once a place of punishment for Rome's worst criminals sentenced to hard labor in mines, is where John penned the book of Revelation.

Domitian was convinced that his rule would be everlasting, but his excessive pride and erratic behavior started to have consequences and he was assassinated in his own home. In fact, he was so hated by the people that upon his death, his name was to be permanently erased from public records and inscriptions, his coins were to be collected and melted down, and his statues were to be smashed.

Even in the dire circumstances of his island prison, John received a profound spiritual reminder of the temporary nature of worldly power and authority. The everlasting kingdom belongs only to one, and when he rules the world, there will be no more crime, warfare, corruption, poverty, or injustice. Jesus is the good, wise, and just King who will reign forever and ever in eternal peace and righteousness.

Saturday, Day 4
REFLECTION DAY

Listen to your favorite version of the "Hallelujah Chorus" while reading the lyrics.

Among all the lines in the hymn, which one resonates with you the most? It could be one from this week's devotional or a new one. Write it in the space below.

Think about a relevant Bible passage that corresponds to this line, and write it in the space provided.

Explain your reasoning for connecting the Bible passage with the verse you provided.

"CHRIST THE LORD IS RISEN TODAY"—A HISTORY

I n the past, it was customary for all Christian churches, regardless of denomination and belief, to perform one specific ritual to begin the service on Easter morning. This ritual is certainly not mentioned in Scripture nor is it likely to be found in any church leadership book. Its absence, however, would have been glaringly obvious. Of course, I'm referring to the singing of Charles Wesley's famous hymn, "Christ the Lord Is Risen Today."

"Christ the Lord Is Risen Today," often referred to as the resurrection hymn, is one of the most well-known and beloved Easter hymns, most likely because it perfectly captures the spirit of the season. For over two hundred fifty years, its resounding alleluias have echoed throughout churches around the world, marking the beginning of Easter services. The hymn is so closely tied to Easter morning that it has become inseparable in the minds of many.

How did one hymn manage to capture the essence of Easter morning and become the anthem that sets the tone for the day? The exact origins of the hymn's ascent to prominence remain somewhat of a mystery. Interestingly enough, it was only after one significant modification to the lyrics and a new tune that it gained immense popularity and became a must-have for honoring the risen Savior. Regrettably, Wesley never had the opportunity to hear the hymn in its current form as the alterations occurred nearly fifty years after he passed away.

Charles Wesley is widely regarded as the greatest hymn writer in history, with a staggering 6,500 hymns to his name. Raised in a Christian household, he and his brother John were the founders of the "Holy Club" at Oxford. In 1735 the Church of England sent them to America to serve as missionaries among the Native Americans, but his evangelistic endeavors were cut short as he wrestled with his own personal conviction of being a child of God himself.

In the spring of 1738, he arrived back home to England, weighed down by disappointment and a sense of failure after abandoning his dream of becoming a successful missionary. As depression took hold, he delved into Scripture for months, seeking a greater understanding of God's grace and mercy. On Sunday, May 21 of that same year, something remarkable happened in that he experienced his own personal revival.

The fire of the Holy Spirit deeply moved him that day, and he documented this remarkable experience in his journal: "At nine, my brother and some friends came and sang a hymn to the Holy Ghost. In about half an hour, they went. I betook myself to prayer. Yet still the Spirit of God strove with my own and the evil spirit till by degrees He chased away the darkness of my unbelief. I found myself convinced and fell into intercession." Less than a year after his conversion and to commemorate his powerful spiritual rebirth, Wesley wrote, "Christ the Lord Is Risen Today."

The song, originally titled "Hymn for Easter Day," uniquely captures the theological significance of the cross and resurrection. Wesley seems to have drawn inspiration from a fourteenth century Latin hymn titled "Jesus Christ Is Risen Today." He would have been familiar with the anonymous hymn since it was included in the *Lyra Davidica*, a collection of hymns and tunes that was initially published in 1708. While the first verse of this ancient hymn may have provided the foundation for Wesley's new creation, the two versions are clearly distinct.

The song was first performed on Easter Sunday in 1739 at the Wesleyan Chapel in London, England. This chapel, also known as the Foundry Meeting House, was a converted iron foundry that Wesley purchased to accommodate his expanding congregation.

That same year, Charles and his brother John published their first hymnal of 223 pages and 239 hymns, entitled *Hymns and Sacred Poems*. There were fifty original hymns by Charles Wesley, which included "Hymn for Christmas-Day," commonly known as "Hark! The Herald Angels Sing," and "Hymn for Easter-Day," which we sing as "Christ the Lord Is Risen Today."

Over the next thirty years, the hymn was published in other hymnals, including *A Collection of Hymns for the Use of the People Called Methodists*, *Harmonia Sacra*, and *Psalms and Hymns*. Surprisingly, Wesley's original composition was not an instant success. Even Charles's brother, John, deliberately left it out of his newly published *Wesleyan Hymn Book* in 1780. From the time it was written, it would take nearly a century for Wesley's hymn to find its rightful place, going through multiple changes and even a new melody to unlock its true potential.

There is uncertainty surrounding the original tune that Wesley had in mind while creating the hymn. Nonetheless, in 1831, a revised version of the hymn was included in a supplement to the *Wesleyan Hymn Book*. An unknown editor made the choice to replace Wesley's original tune for the hymn with the "Easter Hymn" melody that had long been associated with "Jesus Christ Is Risen Today." The only challenge was that the words didn't seem to fit within the structure of the melody.

Fortunately for the editor, it was an Easter song, which sparked an idea for solving his problem. He would simply add a joyful "alleluia" to the end of each line. This seemed logical given the familiar call and response used by early Christians that had continued to that day: "Alleluia! He is risen! Alleluia! He is risen indeed!" The hymn underwent a complete transformation as the lyrics resounded with "alleluias" twenty-four times.

And that was not the only change he made. The original version of Wesley's hymn had eleven stanzas, which were reduced to six and later trimmed down to four. The alterations made to both the melody and the lyrics resulted in the version's creation we are all familiar with and sing today. In fact, it would be hard to imagine singing the hymn without the "alleluias"!

Regarded as one of the most magnificent and cherished hymns ever written, "Christ the Lord Is Risen Today" continues to captivate hearts every Easter morning to this day. Maybe it's because of its uplifting and joyful call to worship, complete with a heartfelt chorus of alleluias that seems to encourage people of all ages to joyfully sing out with all their might. Yet the hymn holds a deeper meaning beyond a mere catchphrase added to enhance the melody. Digging deeper, one uncovers intriguing layers of theology that vividly depict the resurrection and crucifixion, offering profound insights into God's sacrifice for us.

Perhaps, like me, you have cherished memories of joining your voice with others, singing the opening line of this hymn in an Easter sunrise service. Or maybe you're new to the faith, but for some reason, when you hear Wesley's masterpiece sung, a sense of familiarity washes over you. I think that's why this hymn has been used by churches for hundreds of years to open their Easter services—to remind everyone of the purpose behind their gathering on that specific morning. That purpose is to vividly retell the story of the Resurrection, allowing ourselves to be fully absorbed in the experience as if we were eyewitnesses and, most importantly, to rejoice in the triumph of the resurrected Lord Jesus Christ! Alleluia!

"Christ the Lord Is Risen Today" Lyrics

Christ the Lord is risen today, Alleluia!
Sons of men and angels say: Alleluia!
Raise your joys and triumphs high, Alleluia!
Sing, ye heav'ns, and earth, reply: Alleluia!

(Depending on your hymnal, the third verse sometimes comes before this verse.)
Lives again our glorious King, Alleluia!
Where, O death, is now thy sting? Alleluia!
Dying once He all doth save, Alleluia!
Where thy victory, O grave? Alleluia!

Love's redeeming work is done, Alleluia!
Fought the fight, the battle won, Alleluia!
Death in vain forbids Him rise, Alleluia!
Christ hath opened Paradise, Alleluia!

Soar we now where Christ has led, Alleluia!
Following our exalted Head, Alleluia!
Made like Him, like Him we rise, Alleluia!
Ours the cross, the grave, the skies, Alleluia!

(Many hymnals do not contain the fifth and sixth verses.)
Hail the Lord of earth and heaven, Alleluia!
Praise to thee by both be given, Alleluia!
Thee we greet triumphant now, Alleluia!
Hail the Resurrection, thou, Alleluia!

King of glory, soul of bliss, Alleluia!
Everlasting life is this, Alleluia!
Thee to know, thy power to prove, Alleluia!T
hus to sing, and thus to love, Alleluia!

"Christ the Lord Is Risen Today" Wesley Version

"Christ the Lord is ris'n to-day,"
Sons of Men and Angels say!
Raise your Joys and Triumphs high,
Sing ye Heav'ns, and Earth reply.

Love's Redeeming Work is done,
Fought the Fight, the Battle won,
Lo! our Sun's Eclipse is o'er,
Lo! He sets in Blood no more.

Vain the Stone, the Watch, the Seal;
Christ hath burst the Gates of Hell!
Death in vain forbids his Rise:
Christ hath open'd Paradise!

Lives again our glorious King,
Where, O Death, is now thy Sting?
Once He died our Souls to save,
Where thy Victory, O Grave?

Soar we now, where Christ has led,
Following our Exalted Head,
Made like Him, like Him we rise:
Ours the Cross; the Grave; the Skies.

What tho' once we perish'd All,
Partners of our Parent's Fall,
Second Life we All receive,
In our Heav'nly Adam live.

Ris'n with Him, we upward move,
Still we seek the Things above,
Still pursue, and kiss the Son,
Seated on his Father's Throne;

Scarce on Earth a Thought bestow,
Dead to all we leave below,
Heav'n our Aim, and lov'd Abode,
Hid our Life with Christ in God!

Hid; 'till Christ our Life appear,
Glorious in his Members here:
Join'd to Him, we then shall shine
All Immortal, all Divine!

Hail the Lord of Earth and Heav'n!
Praise to Thee by both be giv'n:
Thee we greet Triumphant now;
Hail the Resurrection Thou!

King of Glory, Soul of Bliss,
Everlasting Life is This,
Thee to know, thy Pow'r to prove,
Thus to sing, and thus to love!

Tuesday, Day 6

CHRIST THE LORD IS RISEN TODAY

The angel said to the women, "Do not be afraid, for I know that you are looking for Jesus, who was crucified. He is not here; he has risen, just as he said. Come and see the place where he lay.
Matthew 28:5–6 NIV

Rarely do we wake up with the awareness that the events of today could alter the course of our lives forever. I don't expect that Mary Magdalene did either on that first Easter morning. Not that she hadn't experienced some truly amazing days since Jesus first entered her life and expelled seven demons living inside her... Yes, that was truly a remarkable day that would forever alter the course of her life, filling her with a newfound sense of hope and purpose.

However, there had also been difficult days, such as the tragic events that occurred on the Friday immediately preceding Easter morning. Little did Mary know when she awoke that morning that her day would suddenly take a tragic turn. She couldn't have anticipated the wave of helplessness that would wash over her as she stood at the cross. Even as her eyes were desperate to escape the gruesome sight, her ears were filled with the mocking voices of cruel onlookers urging him to save himself. Throughout it all, a flicker of hope burned inside her, believing that he would. That is, until a guard stabbed him with a spear. Then she knew it was over. It was yet another day that would forever transform her life.

When Mary awoke early Sunday morning, the weight of those memories flooded her mind. Tears streamed down her face as a heavy weight settled in her chest, filling her with despair. What would become of her life now? The one hope she had was lying dead in a borrowed tomb.

When she and the other women began their journey to the tomb that morning, Mary anticipated nothing remarkable happening that day. Suddenly, and without warning, they felt the earth violently shake under their feet. As the women rushed toward the tomb, their hearts pounding in their chests, they were greeted by a breathtakingly radiant angel. The angel was dressed in pure white and had pushed aside the stone blocking the entrance to the tomb and was perched upon it. He comforted the women, telling them not to fear, as Jesus had indeed risen from the dead, fulfilling his promise.

In an unexpected twist on her day, Mary's heart overflowed with awe and great joy as she hurried from the tomb to share the news with the disciples—and for good reason. She knew that the events of the day would have a lasting impact on her life and the lives of many others. However, she probably had no inkling of the profound historical significance of that day, as countless individuals over the next two thousand years would place their faith in exactly what the angel had told her.

The most important fact of the Bible is the angel's declaration to the women that day that Christ had risen from the dead. Scripture tells us that the Lord is faithful to his Word, and his mercies are new every morning.[1] We are recipients of that mercy because the Lord faithfully fulfilled his promise, just as he said he would. Regardless of what you woke up to this morning, the absence of the stone at the tomb's entrance is a constant reminder of hope and the Lord's promise to you. Because of this, we have the reason to sing with joy, not just on Easter morning but every day of the week, that Christ the Lord has risen today!

---

1. Lamentations 3:22–23

Wednesday, Day 7

WHERE, O DEATH, IS NOW THY STING?

Death is swallowed up in victory. O death, where is thy sting? O grave, where is thy victory? 1 Corinthians 15:54–55 KJV

It's not unusual to have a sense of worry or apprehension regarding death and dying. Being alive in our physical bodies is the only state we have ever experienced, and the idea of being in any other state can be somewhat frightening. It's estimated that approximately ten percent of people suffer from thanatophobia, a fear so intense that it cripples them when confronted with the idea of death or the dying process. This condition, also known as "death anxiety," can cause individuals to worry about the nature of their death, whether it will be accompanied by pain, what will happen to their loved ones, or what occurs in the afterlife.

In this passage, the Apostle Paul encourages us to adopt a different mindset toward death. However, his approach may seem unconventional, as he not only claims Christians have victory over death but also appears to mock it.

Paul depicts death as an evil entity with a venomous sting whose sole desire is to inject sin into all creation. Not only does this injection cause physical death but it also leads to spiritual death by separating us from God. The roots of this sting can be traced back to the Garden of Eden, where sin entered humanity when Adam disobeyed God, essentially causing him to be "stu ng."[1] The sting he experienced had far-reaching consequences for him as well as those who would inherit it. Because of Adam's sin, people now must confront the reality of both physical and spiritual death, a fate that could have been avoided had he never sinned. Death exists only because sin warrants it.

Paul does not leave us without hope, as he assures us that, as believers, death does not have the final say. When Christ died on the cross and was resurrected three days later, he achieved victory over Satan, death, and sin. As believers, when we are united with him in his death, we will also be united with him in his resurrection.[2] Thus, those that have unwavering faith need not fear death or the grave, for Jesus has conquered them, eliminating sin's painful sting.

As Christians, we should view death not as a punishment for sin but as the last step toward attaining a glorified body reflecting that of Christ. The promise of eternal life through Jesus gives each of us the confidence to face death without fear, knowing that it's not the end. Death is merely a means for God to draw us nearer to him. In Christ, believers are victorious. So, death, where is thy sting?

---

1. Romans 5:12

2. Romans 6:5

FOUGHT THE FIGHT THE BATTLE WON

I have told you these things so that in me you may have peace. You will have suffering in this world. Be courageous! I have conquered the world. John 16:33 CSB

The crowd erupted as Babe Ruth, the legendary baseball player for the New York Yankees, stepped up to the plate during game three of the 1932 World Series in Chicago. With one home run already under his belt, he watched two balls and two strikes fly by as the Chicago Cubs' bench mercilessly heckled him. Then, as if he had special insight, he extended two fingers toward center field and crushed the next pitch, sending it soaring into the center field seats for a home run. Whether or not Babe had actually called his shot, the event would be forever etched in baseball folklore.

Similarly, when Jesus addressed his disciples, his deliberate use of the phrase "I have" instead of "I will" to describe his victory over the world was as if he were confidently stepping up to the plate and pointing toward the center field seats. This was despite the fact that at this point, he hadn't experienced the anguish of his trial in the Garden of Gethsemane, the injustice of being falsely accused and arrested, or the heartbreak of being abandoned by his disciples. Nor had the Jews and Romans beaten and mocked him or subjected him to the brutal torture of crucifixion, treating him like an ordinary criminal. His Father had not yet forsaken him, and he hadn't felt the weight of the world's sins on his shoulders. He had neither suffered a cruel death nor been laid to rest in a borrowed tomb under the watch of soldiers. Most importantly, he had not triumphed over sin and death by rising from the dead. And yet Jesus still boldly proclaimed that he had already conquered the world.

Jesus had made similar statements before. For example, Jesus told Mary after the death of her brother Lazarus that he was the resurrection and the life.[1] And why shouldn't Jesus make such bold claims when he was also claiming to be one with the Father?[2] Moreover, if we accept John's testimony that Jesus is the Word and was with God from the beginning, then Jesus must have known about the book of life of the Lamb who was slain, a book that was written at the world's creation.[3]

So what is the main message Jesus was trying to convey to his disciples back then and to us now? That it's futile to keep battling against the forces of this world on our own, because we are bound to be defeated every time. But his victory was already guaranteed, an outcome predetermined since the dawn of time. He was simply stepping up to the plate and pointing his fingers toward the center field bench. Best of all, we don't have to overcome the world, because Jesus already did. His promise

---

1. John 11:25

2. John 10:30

3. John 1:1, Revelation 13:8

of a certain future for us is firmly grounded in his resurrection, which offers a hope that is alive and unchanging.[4]

---

4. 1 Peter 1:3–4

Friday, Day 9

KING OF GLORY, SOUL OF BLISS

Who is this King of glory? The Lord, strong and mighty, the Lord, mighty in battle. Psalm 24:8 NIV

According to ancient rabbinical sources, Psalm 24 is considered an "entrance liturgy" that is traditionally sung when entering the presence of God. This psalm is widely attributed to King David, who is said to have composed it as a joyful tribute to the grand entrance of the Ark of the Covenant into Jerusalem. Regardless of its origin, it became designated as the Psalm of the Day in Jewish liturgies for the first day of the week, which is Sunday. On this day, priests would recite the psalm in the temple, and observant Jews would also replicate this practice in their own homes.

Centuries later, there would be another grand entrance into Jerusalem on a Sunday. While the transportation of the ark into the city held great significance, nothing could surpass the sight of the "King of Glory" riding a donkey and ascending the rugged path into Jerusalem. On that particular Sunday, the Jewish people were fully embracing the heart of the psalm by gathering along the streets outside the city walls, waving palm branches, and joyfully exclaiming, "Hosanna to the Son of David! Blessed is the one who comes in the name of the Lord! Hosanna in the highest heaven!"[1]

However, this psalm didn't evoke the same emotional response in everyone's hearts. Interestingly, amid the shouts of jubilation outside the temple, the priests inside would have been solemnly reciting this psalm from a sense of duty rather than with enthusiasm. In fact, days later, they would conspire to have the "King of Glory" executed as a blasphemer. They were in the very presence of "the Lord, who is strong and mighty," and they failed to recognize it.

According to Paul, Jesus is the Lord of glory.[2] As Christians, we are fortunate to have the opportunity to regularly encounter this glory through the presence of the Holy Spirit within us and the ongoing revelation we receive from Scripture. Additionally, as we as believers mature in our relationship with Christ, we are designed to mirror God's glory to the world

It's a sad reality that like the priests, we can recite the appropriate Bible verses, sing songs of worship, and be in the company of other believers yet still fail to recognize the presence of the King of Glory among us. Each day we should strive to feel the same joy and enthusiasm as those that celebrated Jesus on that first Palm Sunday as we constantly grow to be more like him and reflect his presence.

---

1. Matthew 21:9

2. 1 Corinthians 2:8

Saturday, Day 10
REFLECTION DAY

Listen to your favorite version of "Christ the Lord Is Risen Today" while reading the lyrics.

Among all the lines in the hymn, which one resonates with you the most? It could be one from this week's devotional or a new one. Write it in the space below.

Think about a relevant Bible passage that corresponds to this line, and write it in the space provided.

Explain your reasoning for connecting the Bible passage with the line you provided.

Free Discussion Questions Available at
www.BrownChairBooks.com/Free-Resources-Sign-Up.

Monday, Day 11
"HE LIVES"—A HISTORY

O n the evening of Easter 1932, Alfred Ackley anxiously paced back and forth in his study. Despite delivering what he considered to be his finest Easter sermon as the church's pastor, he couldn't help but feel that something was lacking. He could passionately preach from the gospel about the resurrection of Jesus Christ, but he believed there was still something more to the story.

What about his own personal experience with the risen Lord? How should he go about conveying the message that Jesus is alive today? He settled into his desk, pen in hand, and wrote with focused determination. Soon after, he transitioned to the piano as the melody seemed to effortlessly come alive. What eventually emerged became one of the twentieth century's most cherished hymns.

Born in 1887 in Spring Hill, Pennsylvania, Alfred Ackley displayed remarkable musical talent during his formative years. Growing up, his father, a Methodist minister and musician, played a crucial role in his son's education by tutoring him and providing a strong musical foundation. From a young age, he started composing songs, leading him to pursue a musical education in New York City. Eventually he enrolled in the Royal Academy of Music in London, where he honed his skills as a cellist and pianist.

Ackley's journey took a turn when he felt a calling to the pastorate. He made his way back to the States and enrolled at

Westminster Theological Seminary in Princeton, New Jersey. Following his graduation from seminary, Ackley became a Presbyterian minister in 1914 and served as a pastor in churches in both Wilkes-Barre and Elmhurst, Pennsylvania. Together with his older brother, Bentley, he also assisted in performing music for the revivals led by famed evangelist Billy Sunday and his music director, Homer Rodeheaver.

Rodeheaver quickly recognized Ackley's talents as a prolific musician, composer, and editor and hired him to work at his music publishing company. Alfred's impressive body of work included over 1,500 hymns, gospel songs, children's songs, secular songs, and college glee club songs. He also played a significant role in compiling songs and hymns for numerous hymnals. Later in life, he would be awarded an honorary Doctor of Sacred Music degree from John Brown University in recognition of his contributions in the field. However, Ackley's crowning achievement in music would not come until after accepting a call to preach in Escondido, California.

In 1932 Ackley had been preaching a series of revivals at his new church and couldn't help but notice a dedicated young college student who showed up day after day. Following one service, this man, who was a Jew, stayed behind and directly confronted Alfred by boldly asking, "Why should I worship a dead Jew?" Without hesitation, Ackley passionately responded, exclaiming, "He lives! I tell you; He is not dead but lives here and now! Jesus Christ is more alive today than ever before. I can prove it by my own experience, as well as the testimony of countless thousands!"

Days passed, but Ackley couldn't stop thinking about the conversation with the young man. Later that same week, on Easter Sunday morning, he woke up early and switched on the radio while shaving. As he listened to a special Easter broadcast by a well-known liberal preacher from New York City, a wave of anger washed over him.

"Good morning!" began the preacher. "It's Easter! You know, folks, it really doesn't make any difference to me if Christ be risen or not. As far as I am concerned, His body could be as dust in some Palestinian tomb. The main thing is His truth goes marching on!"

Without thinking, Ackley erupted in anger and shouted, "That's a lie!" before hurling the radio across the room. Startled by the commotion and her husband's raised voice, his wife ran into the room. "Why are you shouting?" she asked, thinking something was terribly wrong. In disbelief, he recounted the outrageous words of the fraudulent preacher and then filled her in on the unexpected encounter with the Jewish college student earlier in the week. While he might empathize with the young man's lack of knowledge, the preacher should have certainly known better. Ackley firmly believed that our faith is built upon the conviction that Jesus, who rose from the dead, is alive and active in the world today.

As he made his way to the church that morning, his anger melted away, replaced by a growing sense of anticipation and enthusiasm. He couldn't wait to share his sermon on the resurrection of Jesus on this special Easter day. He delivered it with fiery conviction, firmly believing that it was one of his most powerful sermons to date. However, his enthusiasm would not last as his wife found him restlessly pacing in his study later that same evening. His soul felt burdened, caught between the heartfelt words of his new Jewish friend and the misleading sermon he had heard on the radio. He admitted to her that he hadn't fully expressed everything he wanted to say about the resurrection. In response, she suggested that he should do what he did best and write a song about it.

In his study, Ackley took out the Gospel of Mark and read the account of Christ's resurrection once again. Before long, words started pouring out, effortlessly flowing onto the page in front of him. After a short while, he settled down at the piano, using it to enhance his words with a beautiful melody. It was that very night when Ackley, inspired by his personal encounter with the resurrected Savior, composed his crowning achievement in hymn writing, "He Lives." He then skillfully paired it with the timeless melody, just as it appears in our hymnals today.

The Rodeheaver Company published the hymn, "He Lives," for the first time in their hymnal, *Triumphant Service Songs*, in 1933. The song, serving as a reminder of one's personal experience with the resurrected Savior, has become a timeless anthem sung and played in churches on Easter Sunday around the world. However, it's interesting to note that not everyone valued the individual testimony that forms the foundation of Ackley's hymn. Critics argued that there's not enough evidence of the resurrection in the hymn, leaving it verifiable only by those that claim to have felt the presence of Christ in their hearts.

The Rodeheaver Company tried to address the issue surrounding Ackley's hymn. In a statement, they said, "The scriptural evidence, his own heart, and the testimony of history matched the glorious experience of an innumerable cloud of witnesses that 'He Lives,' so he sat down at the piano and voiced that conclusion in song."

Although Ackley's hymn doesn't recount the biblical story of resurrection, it does provide insight into another Christian experience. The Apostle Paul elaborates on this personal experience, expressing, "I am crucified with Christ; and it is no longer

I who live, but it is Christ who lives in me" and "that Christ may make His home in your hearts through faith."[1]

It's true that we should always be ready to explain the reason for our hope in Christ when someone asks.[2] Our faith is not based on subjective experience but grounded in the unchanging truths of Scripture. However, "He Lives" was not intended to be an intellectual argument or an attempt to address a theological question. It held personal significance for Ackley. He was sincerely trying to answer a question from a young Jewish man about why he should worship someone who was dead. We hear Ackley's response booming through his chorus: "He Lives! He Lives! Christ Jesus Lives Today!" Christ is not dead! He's very much alive, both two thousand years ago and today. It was Ackley's firm conviction that Christians ought to be able to affirm the resurrection of Jesus based on scriptural evidence as well as the impact of Christ in their own lives.

Ackley's method might not win over the average theologian, but for nearly a century, "He Lives" has given voice to countless believers in expressing their own personal experience with the risen Savior.

---

1. Galatians 2:20, Ephesians 3:17

2. 1 Peter 3:15

"He Lives" Lyrics

I serve a risen Savior, He's in this world today;
I know that He is living, whatever men may say.
I see His hands of mercy, I hear His voice of cheer;
And just the time I need Him, He's always near.

Chorus:
He lives! He lives! Christ Jesus lives today!
He walks with me and talks with me, along life's narrow way.
He lives! He lives! Salvation to impart;
You ask me how I know He lives?He lives within my heart!

In all the world around me I see His loving care,
And though my heart grows weary, I never will despair.
I know that He is leading through all the stormy blast;
The day of His appearing will come at last.

Rejoice, rejoice, O Christians, lift up your voice and sing
Eternal hallelujahs to Jesus Christ the King!
The Hope of all who seek Him, the Help of all who find,
None other is so loving, so good and kind.

Tuesday, Day 12

I SERVE A RISEN SAVIOR. HE'S IN THE WORLD TODAY.

I have been crucified with Christ, and I no longer live, but Christ lives in me. The life I now live in the body, I live by faith in the Son of God, who loved me and gave himself for me. Galatians 2:20 CSB

The unbeliever might find it difficult to understand the Christian's claim that Jesus is alive in our world today. Typically when someone dies, they do not return to life. Yet Scripture tells us that approximately five hundred people in the first century witnessed the resurrected Jesus.[1] However, some still find it difficult to fully grasp the concept of a dead person returning to life.

What the skeptic might find easier to believe is the concept of someone's values "living on through another person." For example, we might say that one man's generosity lives on through his children. In other words, the death of one person can greatly influence the life of another, and their memory will

---

1. 1 Corinthians 15:6

persist through this other individual's actions and choices. This, however, is not what the Christian intends when claiming that Christ is alive in the world today. Let's be clear—we're saying unequivocally that Jesus is alive! But more precisely, his Spirit is alive inside all believers.

How is this possible? According to the Apostle John, Jesus, referred to as the Word, ushered in creation at the dawn of time. Then, at just the right time, the Word transformed into a man and entered the confines of time to experience the presence of His creation firsthand and, above all, save them from themselves.[2] Sadly, his own creation turned against him and ultimately killed him. But God raised Christ from the dead, and for the next forty days, his resurrected body walked among the living before ascending to heaven.

At this stage, the skeptic might question how Jesus could still be alive today if his physical body is gone, regardless of whether he was alive when he left. Interestingly, Jesus told his followers that it was to their advantage for him to depart physically, as the Helper would not arrive otherwise.[3] Confined to a physical body, Jesus could only be present in a single location at any given moment. But the Helper, also known as the Holy Spirit, would be with them always, ensuring that they would forget none of his teachings.

But how does this happen? Paul explains in Galatians that a profound transformation takes place when a believer encounters the cross. In exchange for our old sinful life, Jesus offers us a new life, where he lives within us and, over time, transforms

2. John 1

3. John 16:7

us into becoming more like him.[4] This is how Jesus is alive in the world today—his Spirit is living through his followers, who embody his love, practice his teachings, and spread his message! Our lives are no longer under our control; they are now devoted to following Jesus, guided by the Spirit rather than pursuing our own ambitions. So yes, Jesus is very much alive in the world today, his daily presence felt through the faith and devotion of people just like yourself.

---

4. Galatians 2:20

Wednesday, Day 13

HE WALKS WITH ME AND TALKS WITH ME, ALONG LIFE'S NARROW WAY

You can enter God's Kingdom only through the narrow gate. The highway to hell is broad, and its gate is wide for the many who choose that way. But the gateway to life is very narrow and the road is difficult, and only a few ever find it. Matthew 7:13–14 NLT

There are really only two choices in life: follow God's path or choose our own path. While our path appears easy and wide, God's path is more demanding, is narrow, and requires more of us. The difficulty arises because in order to take God's path, we must completely abandon our own.

This raises the question: If our path is so much easier, why not simply choose it instead of following God's? After all, creating your own path in life means tailoring it to your unique aspirations and dreams. It's the life we crave, the life we think we've earned through our relentless toil and sacrifices, a life we imagine as flawlessly fulfilling. We convince ourselves that this path, while not perfect, has its share of good moments. In fact, we're certain the positive experiences will ultimately overshadow any negative ones.

Based solely on this information, the choice seems clear-cut. However, Jesus aimed to shed light on a crucial detail we often conveniently leave out: the destination of our path. In his teachings, Jesus sought to reassure his disciples, many of whom had sacrificed their own paths to follow his, that their choice was a sound one. His response was blunt and direct. Choosing God's way, though hard, leads to life. Choosing your own way, though seemingly easy, ultimately leads to destruction.

Knowing Jesus was personally guiding them, the disciples felt protected from the pitfalls and dangers they might encounter. However, their reassurance crumbled when Jesus informed them he would soon depart. But he reassured them, saying that his departure was crucial for the Holy Spirit to come and serve as their new guide.[1] What's more, the Spirit's guidance would be with them every second of every day, a beacon of light in the darkest moments of their hard journeys.

As we follow the narrow path of Jesus, we are never truly alone. First, we have Jesus, present as the Holy Spirit, walking alongside us. As the narrow way unfolds before us, we rely on prayer and Scripture to communicate with him, prompting us to choose the right direction in order to live a life aligned with his values, even when it's not easy. Second, we are blessed with the company of fellow believers, their lives intertwined with ours, as God uses them to bring us comfort and hope on our journeys. While our individual paths as believers may differ, we all ultimately reach the same destination, guided by God's divine purpose.

---

1. John 16:13

Let's face it—the narrow way is hard, but we deceive ourselves into believing that our own path is risk-free. Select the
path that, while challenging, offers a clear instruction manual
and a dedicated guide to help you navigate through the tough
stretches of life.

Thursday, Day 14

IN ALL THE WORLD AROUND ME I SEE HIS LOVING CARE

Jesus said to them, "My Father is always at his work to this very day, and I too am working." John 5:17 NIV

D o you notice the signs of God's presence in the world around you? It's understandable for non-believers to question God's presence in the world as they haven't experienced him personally. It's ironic, though, that even as people of faith, we sometimes struggle to see God's hand in the events of every day. Even with regular church attendance, Bible study, morning devotions, and prayer, we might still struggle to see tangible evidence of God's work around us.

Anton Chekhov, a celebrated Russian playwright and short story writer, offered a timeless insight: "Knowledge is of no value unless you put it into practice." A brain surgeon can have a deep understanding of the brain, but their experience is limited until they actually perform surgery. I don't know about you, but if I needed brain surgery, I'd want someone who's done it a thousand times before! Likewise, when seeking wisdom for crucial life decisions, you turn to a mature Christian who truly embodies their faith, not just someone who knows the Bible well.

As the Word of God, Jesus undeniably possessed great knowledge. However, when you read the gospels, you discover that Jesus always worked but not in the traditional sense of a job or physical labor. Rather, he deliberately put himself in positions where God could use him. One day, while teaching his disciples, Jesus explained that he was always working because his Father was constantly at work too. Jesus never questioned the presence of God in the world, for he could witness the signs everywhere.

If we, as believers filled with the Holy Spirit, are unable to see God working, then the fault may lie with us. Generally, we are so caught up in our own lives that we fail to notice the countless ways God is working around us. We're not searching for it nor are we listening for it.

So how can we prevent ourselves from missing out on God's work and presence in our lives? Henry Blackaby, author of the bestselling book *Experiencing God*, advised, "Watch and see where God is working and then join him there." It's not enough to just know things; we need to actually use that knowledge in real situations. We can start by having spiritual conversations with those that don't share our beliefs, doing kind things for strangers, or volunteering outside of church. Most importantly, pray for God to give you eyes to see and ears to hear; then watch for those opportunities to appear. He will not let you down!

I KNOW THAT HE IS LEADING THROUGH ALL THE STORMY BLAST

He got up, rebuked the wind and said to the waves,
"Quiet! Be still!" Then the wind died down and it
was completely calm. Mark 4:39 NIV

The Sea of Galilee is fifteen miles long, is eight miles wide, sits six hundred feet below sea level, and is surrounded by steep hills. It's not unusual for powerful gusts of wind to develop quickly between the steep cliffs, becoming stronger as they sweep down toward the lake and, within minutes, whipping up powerful waves that crash against anything in their path. This is the type of storm that Jesus and his disciples found themselves in one memorable night.

In Matthew's account, the storm is described using the Greek word "seismos," which is the origin of our word "seismology," the study of earthquakes. In other words, this storm was so monstrous and the waves were so enormous that it smashed into the boat with great force, swamping it with water. It was only a matter of time before they went under. And let's not forget that some of these disciples were experienced fishermen, making them well versed in the lake's ways, and yet the ferocious storm had them fearing for their lives.

This makes one wonder how Jesus could have possibly slept through this! As the boat tossed violently and water gushed in, he laid in the back of the boat on a cushion, sleeping soundly. After being awakened by the disciples' panicked cries, he instantly calmed the raging storm, leaving them in awe. This story rightfully conveys the message that if Jesus has the power to control weather patterns on the Sea of Galilee, he can also bring peace to the storms we face in our own lives. This truth alone is wonderful, but Jesus had more to teach his disciples that day.

As we continue reading the story, we encounter a powerful moment immediately following the storm's fury. Jesus and his disciples found themselves on the shores of Gerasenes, met by a man whose cries and contortions revealed the torment of demons within him. Jesus demonstrated his power by expelling the demons into a herd of pigs. The townspeople, wary and fearful, urged him to leave, so he crossed to the other side of the lake, where he miraculously healed a woman just by her touching his clothing. Jesus further demonstrated his power by miraculously restoring the life of a synagogue leader's deceased daughter. All in a day's work!

In the storm's aftermath, Jesus had confronted his disciples about their wavering faith. Having clearly emphasized his divine authority over natural phenomena, he next wanted to communicate his authority over the supernatural realm, an authority that extended even to life and death. The message Jesus was trying to convey was that there is no force in this world or the next that he did not have power over. He is Lord over all!

We must ask ourselves: Have we reduced Jesus to simply someone who intervenes in emergencies? Our boat feels like it's sinking, and we're desperate to know if he notices or even cares. Jesus will absolutely guide us through life's storms, but he wants us to surrender all parts of our lives to his care. The Jesus who triumphed over death that first Easter morning is the same Jesus who calmed raging storms, drove out evil spirits, restored the sick to health, and brought life back from the dead. May our trust in Jesus reach beyond the storms we face to become the guiding force in every part of our lives.

Saturday, Day 16
REFLECTION DAY

Listen to your favorite version of "He Lives" while reading the lyrics.

Among all the lines in the hymn, which one resonates with you the most? It could be one from this week's devotional or a new one. Write it in the space below.

Think about a relevant Bible passage that corresponds to this line, and write it in the space provided.

Explain your reasoning for connecting the Bible passage with the line you provided.

Monday, Day 17

"THE OLD RUGGED CROSS"—A HISTORY

From Elvis and his rock and roll swagger to Willie Nelson and his country twang, hundreds of artists have recorded "The Old Rugged Cross," solidifying its title for many as the most popular hymn of the twentieth century. The celebrated hymn has appeared in films and television programs and was a regular part of George Beverly Shea's performances at Billy Graham crusades. However, its composer, George Bennard, found writing his most famous hymn to be a struggle. With just the melody and one line written, the rest of the words continued to evade him. He just needed a spark of inspiration to find the perfect words, and that spark would surely come!

Bennard's father was born in the rugged highlands of Scotland in 1837 and immigrated to the United States, eventually settling in Youngstown, Ohio. It was here that his six children would be born, including his only son, George, who was born in 1873. In search of work, his father moved his growing family to Albia, Iowa, a town situated just over sixty miles southeast of Des Moines, and found work in a local tavern. But after the tavern was destroyed by a fire, he moved his family to Lucas, Iowa, and became a coal miner.

The family suffered a terrible loss in 1889 when the elder Bennard died in a coal mining accident. At just sixteen, George faced the enormous responsibility of supporting his mother and five sisters. Just barely over five feet tall, the young man followed in his father's footsteps and worked in the dangerous coal mines each day to provide for his family. Bennard toiled for many grueling years in the coal mines, eventually marrying, yet his future held something other than a life in the mines.

One day in 1895, drawn by curiosity, Bennard walked five long, dusty miles into town to a local Salvation Army meeting. During the passionate, uplifting service, Bennard felt the Holy Spirit move him, and he responded to the speaker's invitation, committing his life to Jesus Christ. In 1898 he and his wife, Ariminda, joined the Salvation Army as brigade officers, spending nearly ten years leading revival meetings across the Midwest. He left the Salvation Army in 1907 and, for the next three decades, traveled as a Methodist revivalist, primarily in Michigan and New York but also in Canada.

In the years that would follow, Bennard and his wife would settle in Albion, Michigan, where he became a skilled hymn writer, producing more than three hundred hymns during his lifetime. Most of his hymns faded into obscurity, lost to the relentless march of time, save for one that caused him intense emotional and spiritual turmoil.

One day in 1912, after long hours of intense study, silent prayer, and deep meditation on the Scriptures, he declared, "I saw the Christ of the cross as if I were seeing John 3:16 leave the printed page, take form, and act out the meaning of redemption. The more I contemplated these truths, the more convinced I became that the cross was far more than just a religious symbol but rather the very heart of the gospel."

As he grappled with this spiritual truth, a melody and the line, "I will cherish the old rugged cross," came to him. He struggled to write the appropriate words to go with it, but few came to mind. For months, that one line consumed him, a constant presence in his heart and mind, crowding out all else.

Bennard continued preaching throughout Michigan and New York, adding bits and pieces to his creation only when inspiration came. Ironically, the cure for his writer's block was to preach the subject he was writing about over and over again. However, during a 1913 revival in Michigan, an event occurred that profoundly affected him spiritually, deepening his understanding of the cross. During one meeting, some teenagers heckled and ridiculed him, mocking the cross and disrupting the service. This caused George to think deeply about the meaning of the cross, the weight of it heavy in his mind as he pictured his Savior carrying the burden of the world's sins for the very people who mocked him.

He came home, placed his song manuscript on the kitchen table, and the words he'd been searching for effortlessly came to him. Calling his wife into the kitchen, he picked up his guitar and sang for her the first couple of stanzas; she loved it and thought it was wonderful. Regarding the hymn, Bennard said, "I composed the melody first. The words that I first wrote were imperfect. The words of the finished hymn were put into my heart in answer to my own need."

Bennard put the finishing touches on the hymn, completing all four stanzas, while staying at the parsonage of his friends, the Reverend and Mrs. Leroy O. Bostwick, during a two-week revival at the First Methodist Episcopal Church in Pokagon. From his penciled notes, he taught the piece to the four-member choir then gave the first public performance of the hymn during a church service, accompanied by a pianist and violinist. The Bostwicks were so moved by the hymn that they happily covered the costs of creating the music plate and printing the first copies.

But before publishing his new creation, he sent the manuscript to Charles Gabriel in Chicago, a leading gospel hymn writer of the day, seeking his expertise in adding chords to the melody. Gabriel did so and returned the document with the message, "You will hear from this song." Later that year, the hymn was introduced at a large Chicago Evangelistic Institute convention, where it quickly gained popularity and soon became well loved throughout the northern states.

The hymn's popularity, however, would explode nationwide by 1915, just two years after its debut, thanks to Billy Sunday's tent revivals and his song leader, Homer Rodeheaver. Around 1920, Bennard sold the song's copyright to Rodeheaver's publishing company for $500, forfeiting any potential future royalties. Years later, in 1938, he received a final payment of $5,000 to renew the copyright as stipulated in the contract. That was all the royalties Bennard received for his work.

That same year, a poll by a national radio network determined that Bennard's hymn was America's favorite song. By 1939 the hymn boasted sales of over fifteen million copies and multiple recordings and soon became one of the most widely published songs throughout America.

Though "The Old Rugged Cross" is one of the world's best loved hymns, it has not been immune from criticism. Some contemporary Christians view it as culturally irrelevant, while others see its emphasis on the cross as misplaced. Bennard, however, remained unfazed, humbly crediting God for his writings and creations, considering himself merely God's instrument. The hymn was his way of grappling with a deep spiritual crisis centered on the cross, the same cross that inspired the hymn's title.

More than a century later, "The Old Rugged Cross" stands firm, its presence felt in the heartfelt choirs of countless churches, the passionate fervor of revivals, and the quiet reverence of countless Easter services affecting millions each year. But even more so, the hymn has resonated deeply with countless seasoned Christians nearing the end of their earthly journeys, who find solace in the prospect of exchanging their cross one day for a crown.

"The Old Rugged Cross" Lyrics

On a hill far away stood an old rugged cross,
the emblem of suffering and shame;
and I love that old cross where the dearest and best
for a world of lost sinners was slain.

Chorus:
So I'll cherish the old rugged cross,
till my trophies at last I lay down;
I will cling to the old rugged cross,
and exchange it some day for a crown.

O that old rugged cross, so despised by the world,
has a wondrous attraction for me;
for the dear Lamb of God left his glory above
to bear it to dark Calvary.

In that old rugged cross, stained with blood so divine,
a wondrous beauty I see,
for 'twas on that old cross Jesus suffered and died,
to pardon and sanctify me.

To that old rugged cross I will ever be true,
its shame and reproach gladly bear;
then he'll call me some day to my home far away,
where his glory forever I'll share.

Tuesday, Day 18

ON A HILL FAR AWAY STOOD AN OLD RUGGED CROSS, THE EMBLEM OF SUFFERING AND SHAME

We must focus on Jesus, the source and goal of our faith. He saw the joy ahead of him, so he endured death on the cross and ignored the disgrace it brought him. Now he holds the honored position—the one next to God the Father on the heavenly throne. Hebrews 12:2 GWT

Crucifixion was a brutal form of capital punishment invented by the Persians and later used by the Romans. Reserved for the worst criminals, the condemned would be nailed to a wooden cross and left to die a slow, agonizing death while exposed to the elements and the jeers of onlookers. In fact, in the early days of Christianity, some people were hesitant to embrace the religion because the cross was considered a symbol of shame and humiliation in Roman society, making it a potentially off-putting symbol for potential converts.

Yet Jesus, the model of our Christian faith, endured the agonizing death of the cross and the physical torment it entailed.
One definition of "endure" is to bear hardship without resistance or with patience. Although the brutality of Jesus' crucifixion—the beatings, the nailing to the cross—was inflicted by
wicked men, we must remember that his sacrifice was freely
given. Twelve legions of angels stood ready at his beck and
call, their power unmatched in this world, should he choose
to summon them. Instead, the Word of God, the Creator of all,
willingly allowed his creation—blinded by hatred—to reject and
crucify him.

Jesus didn't just endure the pain inflicted by the cross but also
willingly chose to ignore the agonizing shame and humiliation
it would bring. Although the cross was a symbol of shame, Jesus
embraced it, refusing to be humiliated or distracted from doing
what God needed him to do. He allowed humanity to despise
him as he bore the weight of their sins. The spotless Lamb of
God, who knew no shame, became shame for them.

What divine purpose and unwavering commitment com-
pelled Jesus to embrace the cross and prioritize selfless love
above the pain and shame inflicted upon him? According to
this passage, he was driven by the joy awaiting him! His faith
rested not only on God's past actions but also on his future ones.
Despite the pain, suffering, humiliation, and shame, he knew
Sunday was coming. Jesus understood his suffering was temporary and that his death and resurrection would bring salvation
and life. And he also knew that he would be restored to his
rightful place of honor with God.

Is your faith based only on what God has done in the past or
what he will do in the future? Even when life is hard and your
faith is mocked, can you still experience joy? It's helpful to be
reminded during these times to keep our eyes focused on Jesus

because Sunday is coming. And on that day, a joy unlike anything you've ever known, a joy that transcends this world, awaits you.

O THAT OLD RUGGED CROSS, SO DESPISED BY THE WORLD, HAS A WONDROUS ATTRACTION FOR ME

For the message of the cross is foolishness to those who are perishing, but to us who are being saved it is the power of God. 1 Corinthians 1:18 NIV

In the time of the Apostle Paul, Corinth was a thriving cosmopolitan city in ancient Greece, a hub of business, transport, and leisure. Yet it was also a center of moral decay, characterized by its rampant immorality. The city even earned the moniker "Sin City," and the phrase "living like a Corinthian" became a byword for a life of excess and depravity. Corinth, however, was also a renowned center of philosophy, celebrated for its intellectual pursuits and lively philosophical discussions. And when Paul arrived in Corinth, there was also a large Jewish community with a prominent synagogue.

This diverse blend of cultures, religions, and knowledge and a cosmopolitan atmosphere presented a significant challenge for the spread of Christianity. During his second missionary journey, Paul spent eighteen months in Corinth, planting a church and becoming intimately familiar with the difficulties that would plague it. Considering this, Paul's first letter to the church strongly encouraged them to avoid worldly pleasures and center their evangelistic message specifically on the crucified Christ.

He undoubtedly realized some would find this message foolish, and he would validate his assertion in the verses to come. For the Jew, Paul explained, the concept would be problematic because they believed the Messiah would miraculously defeat Israel's enemies. And for the Gentiles living in Corinth, the notion of God offering his Son as a sacrifice for humanity would have seemed illogical. From a pagan perspective, the very notion of a god serving mortals, particularly by sacrificing his own life, would be viewed as a clear sign of divine weakness.

I'd argue that Corinth isn't so unlike many of our cities today. To many, the message of the cross sounds foolish, as they view the Bible as old-fashioned and insignificant. Usually it isn't a lack of knowledge but pride that stops them from humbling themselves before Christ and accepting the necessary changes in their lives that he requires. Sadly, others have simply been fooled by the world's meaningless philosophies and traditions.[1]

In the next chapter of Corinthians, Paul would argue that true understanding and acceptance of Jesus Christ's message depend on the work of the Holy Spirit within a person.[2] Therefore, it's hardly surprising that the world views our belief in Jesus' atoning sacrifice on the cross, resulting in forgiveness and salvation for believers, as foolish.

---

1. Colossians 2:8

2. 1 Corinthians 2:14

However, for those that believe, faith in Christ offers a far greater reward than anything this world can offer. Paul's central point is that faith in Christ is a "wondrous attraction" that transcends human religion and wisdom. It's a revolutionary call to change direction in your life, but it demands repentance and a change of heart regarding God and divine matters. And for those that do and believe, it holds extraordinary power and attraction!

Thursday, Day 20

IN THAT OLD RUGGED CROSS, STAINED WITH BLOOD SO DIVINE, A WONDROUS BEAUTY I SEE

Then he took a cup, and when he had given thanks, he gave it to them, saying, "Drink from it, all of you. This is my blood of the covenant, which is poured out for many for the forgiveness of sins. Matthew 26:27–28 NIV

John stood frozen, his heart pounding in his chest as he stared at his friend, the one he believed to be the Messiah, the Son of God, nailed to a cross on the hill called Golgotha outside Jerusalem's city gates. The sounds of the hammering, the shouts of the Roman soldiers, the jeers of hecklers, and the mournful cries of the onlookers created a cacophony of despair that tore at his soul.

The past twenty-four hours had been a whirlwind, starting with the celebration of the most unusual Passover meal he had ever taken part in. If "unusual" was not the right word, then perhaps "unconventional" would be a more fitting description. But hadn't life with Jesus these past few years been exactly that? A shudder ran through him at the image of Jesus, towel at his waist, about to wash their grime-covered feet; the thought was unsettling. The act of humility was almost too much to bear.

A faint smile then creased at the corner of his mouth as he remembered Peter's initial refusal of Jesus' request then his oddly specific declaration to be washed from head to toe. Peter, ever the bold one, was always the first to blurt out the thoughts and feelings they all harbored. He even swore to Jesus that he would follow him to the bitter end and was ready to face death at his side. John scanned the murmuring, restless crowd gathered around the cross, desperately searching for Peter. Where was he? Surely he would be here now...especially now.

His eyes fell again on Jesus and the sight of blood, matted and glistening, dripping from his body onto the splintered cross. Ironically, this horrific scene reminded him of Jesus' words from the previous night's Passover preparation. What was it? Something about his blood being the new covenant for the forgiveness of many sins. While growing up, John had learned during Passover celebrations that the covenant between God and the Jewish people was sealed with the blood of a sacrificial lamb.

What Jesus was describing to his apostles that last evening was God's establishment of a revolutionary new covenant. However, this covenant would extend beyond Israel to encompass all that come to God through faith in Jesus.

Standing at the cross and overwhelmed with his own pain, John may not have fully understood the Passover symbols Jesus had used to describe his coming sacrifice. Later, though, while reflecting on that dark day, John would write that Jesus is the world's light and walking in that light cleanses us from all sin through his divine blood.[1] This potent, life-giving image of Jesus' divine blood serves as a stark reminder that it holds power beyond any darkness we encounter.

---

1. John 1:4, 1 John 1:7

Friday, Day 21

TO THAT OLD RUGGED CROSS I WILL EVER BE TRUE, ITS SHAME AND REPROACH GLADLY BEAR

Then Jesus said to his disciples, "If anyone wants to follow after me, let him deny himself, take up his cross, and follow me. Matthew 16:24 CSB

Jesus frequently used parables that were rich in metaphor to teach his followers, though they were often hard to understand. This, however, was not the case when he told his disciples they would need to take up their cross and follow him. The meaning of Jesus' words this time was clear to all.

In that day, bearing one's cross held no religious or spiritual significance; it served solely as a method of capital punishment. But over the past two thousand years, the cross has undergone a profound shift in its cultural interpretation. Today many believe they are "bearing the cross" of Jesus when worn as a fashion statement—on necklaces, t-shirts, tattoos, and more. Others use "cross bearing" to refer to the petty annoyances or irritations we encounter in life or when trying to limit some destructive behavior or sin. Both examples are a stark contrast to its original intention: the shameful burden carried by a condemned man, like Jesus, to his execution.

While we typically associate bearing one's cross with spiritual burdens, physical hardships can be involved as well. However, in all of history, only one man, Simon, ever physically bore the weight of Jesus' actual cross. The gospels mention him three times, yet his story remains largely unknown.

What we do know is that Simon was a Cyrenian, arriving from the countryside and traveling along the ancient route of the Via Dolorosa. The path, known as the "way of suffering," is traditionally believed to be the one Jesus walked to his crucifixion. Simon must have gotten caught up in the crowds watching a man, bleeding and broken, stumble under the weight of a rough-hewn crossbeam. Suddenly soldiers were upon Simon, yanking him forward. The weight of the crossbeam, bearing the gruesome mark of the injured man's suffering, was painfully thrust onto his own back. The rough wood scraped against his skin as he was forced to walk behind the condemned man to his death.

Clearly Simon didn't want to be there. Who would? In bearing the condemned man's cross, it was almost as if he shared his same punishment and experienced the same shame. He likely wondered what others would think of him now, whether they would look at him with suspicion or scorn. What might they say to him? What relationships, opportunities, or possessions might he now lose because of this decision?

Though all of that might be true, the Gospel of Mark suggests a different outcome might have been possible, perhaps even a more hopeful one. Mark's gospel, unusually, includes the detail that Simon was the father of Alexander and Rufus, men who were likely familiar to Mark's readers.[1] Why bother mentioning them otherwise? Some believe that the Rufus mentioned here is the same man Paul greets in the book of Romans, calling him "chosen in the Lord," and whose mother, perhaps Simon's wife, also cared for Paul.[2] Although the Bible is silent on Simon of Cyrene's life after the Resurrection, tradition paints a vivid picture of him journeying to Egypt, carrying the gospel's message and sharing its hope with the people of that land.

Although you won't physically carry Jesus' cross like Simon did, the cross symbolizes one thing: dying to self. It's a symbol of the shame and humiliation that the Christian must be prepared to endure for the sake of Christ, should it be required. It means sacrificing personal desires to the point of giving up our hopes, dreams, possessions, and even our lives if need be. Yet Jesus assures us that for every sacrifice we make, God's boundless peace and love will bring us a life worth living.

---

1. Mark 15:21

2. Romans 16:13

Saturday, Day 22

REFLECTION DAY

Listen to your favorite version of "The Old Rugged Cross" while reading the lyrics.

Among all the lines in the hymn, which one resonates with you the most? It could be one from this week's devotional or a new one. Write it in the space below.

Think about a relevant Bible passage that corresponds to this line, and write it in the space provided.

Explain your reasoning for connecting the Bible passage with the line you provided.

Free Discussion Questions Available at
www.BrownChairBooks.com/Free-Resources-Sign-Up.

Monday, Day 23

"BLESSED ASSURANCE"—A HISTORY

It was the summer of 1873 as Fanny, a woman in her early fifties, was on her way to her friend Phoebe's grand Fifth Avenue residence in New York City. Despite their different backgrounds, the two women bonded over their shared passion for music and their years of attending the same church. Little did either know that their collaboration around the piano that day would result in one of history's most celebrated hymns.

Frances (Fanny) Jane Crosby, a renowned American poet, hymn writer, and composer, was born in Putnam County, New York, on March 24, 1820, as the only child of John and Mercy Crosby. At only six weeks old, Fanny developed a severe cold that caused her eyes to become inflamed. Her father took her to a poorly trained country doctor, who treated her inflamed eyes with a mustard plaster poultice. The consequences of this decision were catastrophic; she lost her sight completely because of damage to her optic nerve. Six months later, her father died, leaving her mother and grandmother to raise her, a devastating blow that compounded the family's existing hardships.

In order to support the family, her mother spent long hours working as a maid, but her grandmother filled the void, becoming an unforgettable influence in young Fanny's life. Her grandmother's strong faith fueled efforts to dedicate nearly all her time and energy to reading the Bible to Fanny and helping her memorize extensive passages of Scripture. It's been reported that as a young woman, she had committed to memory Genesis through Deuteronomy, Ruth, significant portions of Psalms, Proverbs, Song of Solomon, and much of the New Testament. Her remarkable memory spurred her to poetry, and she wrote her first poem at just eight years old.

At fifteen, Fanny was admitted to the New York Institution for the Blind, where she began her formal education. She excelled academically in English literature, science, philosophy, and music, complemented by a musical talent that extended to the piano, organ, harp, and guitar. Her outstanding academic record led to a teaching position at the institute at twenty-two, immediately after graduation.

In her role as a teacher, she traveled to Washington, DC, to champion education of the blind, achieving a milestone in 1846 as the first woman to address the United States Senate. Following this, she spoke before a joint session of the U.S. Congress to urge support for blind education in Boston, Philadelphia, and New York.

After sixteen years of teaching on staff, she retired and married her classmate and colleague, Alexander Van Alstyne, in 1858. Their mutual love for literature, combined with his musical talent, was a perfect match. Later, they collaborated on many hymns, and he often transcribed his wife's poems since Crosby could not write and composed lyrics entirely in her mind. Though they went on to live a wonderful life together, their only child, a daughter, tragically died in her sleep soon after birth.

Fanny started writing hymns in 1851, a path that would eventually lead her to collaborate with the renowned hymn writer William B. Bradbury in 1864. Their successful songwriting partnership led to a publishing deal with Biglow & Main Publishers. Under her contract, Crosby was obligated to write three hymns a week at a rate of two dollars per hymn. Since Crosby often wrote six or seven hymns a day, this condition posed no difficulty for her. To avoid the impression that they only published Crosby's hymns as many started appearing in denominational hymnals, Biglow & Main credited her work under several pseudonyms.

Crosby's prolific career produced over 8,000 hymns, along with more than 1,000 secular songs, four poetry books, and two best-selling autobiographies, making her America's most renowned hymn writer. Over one hundred million copies of her songs were printed in her lifetime. Frequently a hymn would drift to her ears, and she'd inquire about the author only to discover it was one of her own compositions. Fanny's memory was so phenomenal that on one occasion, she recalled over forty hymns before finding someone to write them down for her. Her accomplishments were certainly impressive, yet it would be her collaboration with a church friend that would produce her most famous hymn.

Phoebe Palmer Knapp composed more than five hundred gospel hymns and tunes. Born in New York City in 1839, she was the daughter of renowned evangelist Dr. Walter Palmer and raised in a home filled with religious music. A natural musical talent blossomed early in her life, eventually establishing her reputation as a renowned composer and poet, especially known for her works for children. At sixteen, she wed Joseph Fairchild Knapp, a Sunday school teacher who later amassed a fortune in publishing before later becoming the second president of the Metropolitan Life Insurance Company. In their New York City home at the Hotel Savoy on Fifth Avenue, the Knapps installed what was then thought to be the largest privately owned pipe organ in a private residence.

Phoebe frequently invited Fanny to her home, just as she did on that summer afternoon in 1873. A catchy tune had been stuck in Phoebe's head all day, so she sat down at the piano and shared the unique melody with her friend. Turning to Fanny, she asked, "What does this tune say to you?" Without hesitation, Fanny replied, "It says, 'Blessed assurance, Jesus is mine, Oh, what a foretaste of glory divine!'" Using her extensive knowledge of Scripture, Fanny then dictated three verses and a chorus that afternoon while Phoebe wrote them down, fitting them to the melody. Within a few hours, the duo had completed "Blessed Assurance" just as we hear it sung today.

The hymn was quickly published in the July 1873 edition of *Palmer's Guide to Holiness and Revival Miscellany*, a magazine printed by Mrs. Knapp's evangelist parent. It became an instant hit as it spread through local churches, gaining popularity among many congregations. A major turning point came when it was published in Ira Sankey's *1887 Gospel Songs, No. 5* as well as becoming a staple in the revivals Sankey and Dwight Moody held throughout Great Britain and America.

Standing the test of time, "Blessed Assurance" has remained a cherished hymn, inspiring and uplifting worshippers across the globe for over one hundred fifty years. Shortly before her ninety-fifth birthday, Fanny passed away. Even though she didn't want a large headstone, a large memorial stone was erected, bearing the inscription: "Blessed assurance, Jesus is mine. Oh, what a foretaste of glory divine." Most who knew Fanny would claim her life was certainly a living testimony to the "blessed assurance" that characterizes a follower of Christ.

"Blessed Assurance" Lyrics

Blessed assurance, Jesus is mine;
Oh, what a foretaste of glory divine!
Heir of salvation, purchase of God,
Born of His Spirit, washed in His blood.

Chorus
This is my story, this is my song,
Praising my Savior all the day long.
This is my story, this is my song,
Praising my Savior all the day long.

Perfect submission, perfect delight,
Visions of rapture now burst on my sight;
Angels descending, bring from above
Echoes of mercy, whispers of love.

Perfect submission, all is at rest,
I in my Savior am happy and blest;
Watching and waiting, looking above,
Filled with His goodness, lost in His love

Tuesday, Day 24

BLESSED ASSURANCE, JESUS IS MINE

For you are saved by grace through faith, and this is not from yourselves; it is God's gift—not from works, so that no one can boast. Ephesians 2:8–9 CSB

A Barna Group study revealed that approximately sixty-five percent of U.S. Christians have wrestled with doubts about their faith, suggesting that questioning one's salvation is a common experience. This doubt seems to stem from several sources, including dwelling on past mistakes and failures, trusting feelings over faith, exposure to unbiblical teachings, or a pattern of habitual sin and disobedience. Others feel trapped into thinking that they are not good enough, while others might be experiencing a season of spiritual drought.

It should be noted that while some doubts are just fleeting thoughts, others might be valid indicators that one is not saved. But the presence or absence of doubt shouldn't determine your assurance of salvation. We might question our faith because we judge it against the inconsistent realities of life—the death of a loved one, the ever-present threat of job loss, the potential for relationship breakdown, or the vulnerability of our health—making faith seem less certain in comparison. In all these examples, subtle doubts can creep into our minds, making us question the eventual outcome.

This is not the sort of salvation assurance found in Scripture. For that, we look to what Fannie Crosby would call a blessed assurance—a holy, unshakeable conviction. It's an assurance free from doubt, a certainty that Jesus is yours. So how can we truly experience this blessed assurance in our own lives?

First, we understand that salvation is a gift from God. We are not entitled to it nor can we earn it based on our own merits, achievements, or goodness. Trusting in Jesus as Savior then allows God's saving grace to flow in, beginning a renewal of one's heart and mind through the Holy Spirit; it is a down payment on God's promise, secured through Jesus' death on the cross.[1] The Holy Spirit assures us of our place in God's family and, with his unbreakable seal upon us, leaves no room for doubt. Author Timothy Keller profoundly wrote, ""

Perhaps not all doubt is bad if it gets you to examine your faith. In fact, Paul urges Christians to honestly examine their lives, urging them to evaluate whether their beliefs and choices truly align with the teachings of Jesus.[2] If you're unsure where to start, follow the advice of King David, and ask God to search your heart, identifying anxious thoughts or anything displeasing to him, and then guide you toward eternal life.[3]

Once you've established evidence of the Holy Spirit's work in your life, stop doubting, and embrace your faith with "blessed assurance."

---

1. Ephesians 1:13–14

2. 2 Corinthians 13:5

3. Psalm 139:23–24

Wednesday, Day 25

BORN OF HIS SPIRIT, WASHED IN HIS BLOOD

Jesus answered, "Truly I tell you, unless someone is born of water and the Spirit, he cannot enter the kingdom of God. Whatever is born of the flesh is flesh, and whatever is born of the Spirit is spirit.
John 3:5–6 CSB

N icodemus was confused. He considered himself an intelligent and capable religious instructor, an influential Pharisee and leader in Israel, adept at explaining the complexities of God's teachings. Yet this seemingly uneducated, itinerant preacher named Jesus had just softly rebuked him for failing to grasp the very subject he was renowned for teaching masterfully. His wounded pride notwithstanding, he acknowledged Jesus' teachings were unique and potentially revolutionary, certainly unlike anything he'd encountered before. He also knew that such teachings, if proven true, would upend his entire belief system.

Sitting across from Jesus one night, Nicodemus opened their conversation by asserting that he knew Jesus' teachings and miracles had to be from God. The compliment, however, didn't impress Jesus. Instead, he shifted tactics, suggesting Nicodemus didn't know what was from God and what wasn't and the only way to know was to be born again, specifically a spiritual rebirth.

Nicodemus's surprised expression prompted Jesus to assure him that the teaching wasn't unexpected; indeed, as a teacher, he should already be familiar with it. But for some reason, Nicodemus wasn't! Now he was struggling to grasp the concept of spiritual rebirth. How could he possibly be born again? The idea sounded utterly foreign to him. Like most Jews of his generation, he believed he'd already experienced new birth, as had all faithful Israelites. This message, if revealed, would challenge the deeply held conviction that Jewish ancestral lineage ensured a place in God's divine kingdom.

Jesus explained to Nicodemus that one's first birth, regardless of heritage, does not guarantee a place in the kingdom; one must be born again but this time of the Spirit. No fallen human, regardless of their ancestry, morality, intelligence, or emotional depth, can enter God's holy presence. Jesus made it clear to Nicodemus that night that the only path was through him, the Son of God.

The metaphor of birth used by Jesus to describe salvation to Nicodemus is fitting as it conveys the idea of a fresh start and new life. Just as you played no part in your physical birth, Jesus highlights that our spiritual rebirth is entirely God's doing, a miraculous act of grace. The moment we place our faith in the risen Christ, a wave of God's grace washes over us, erasing the stain of sin, guilt, and condemnation. Then something amazing happens! The Holy Spirit gives new life, enabling fellowship with God's Spirit and confirming our place in his kingdom.

Thursday, Day 26
VISIONS OF RAPTURE NOW BURST ON MY SIGHT

For we walk by faith, not by sight. 2 Corinthians 5:7
CSB

We commonly use the phrase, "seeing is believing," to convey the idea that proof requires visual confirmation. Fanny Crosby, however, stands out as a notable exception as her life bears witness to our daily Bible verse, "walk by faith, not by sight." Despite being blind from infancy, she lived a life of unwavering faith, viewing her blindness as the greatest gift from God.

Blindness didn't hinder Fanny's prolific output as a hymn writer. Her passion fueled the creation of more than eight thousand hymns, a testament to her faith and the power of her imagination. She is quoted as saying, "If perfect earthly sight were offered to me tomorrow, I would not accept it. I might not have ever sung hymns to the praise of God if I had been distracted by the beautiful and interesting things about me."

A preacher once expressed pity to Fanny, saying it was a shame God hadn't granted her sight. She quickly replied, "Do you know that if at birth I had been able to make one petition, it would have been that I should be born blind?" When the shocked preacher asked why, she said, "Because when I get to heaven, the first face that shall ever gladden my sight will be that of my Savior!"

Perhaps this is the vision Fanny had in mind when she wrote the verse, "Visions of rapture now burst on my sight." One can only imagine what it must feel like to experience sight for the very first time after a lifetime without it. And the glorious vision of your Savior as your very first sight would undoubtedly fill you with pure, ecstatic rapture.

Blindness gave Fanny ample reason to question God's plan. But she never resented her situation, choosing instead, from a young age, to accept her disability as part of God's plan and to not be defeated by it. Fanny's hard work and diligence brought her success in school, teaching, and marriage, yet she didn't find success as a hymn writer until she was in her mid-forties. Back then, she never could have envisioned her future fame, friendships with presidents, and recognition as the "mother of modern congregational singing in America." But Fanny disregarded all that; she yearned only for a vision of her Savior.

As Christians, our lives should reflect our faith in God and his promises, even when, like Fanny, we lack visible proof. Walking by faith is a journey of listening to the Holy Spirit and the Bible, choosing to obey God's will despite our limited understanding.

Friday, Day 27

PERFECT SUBMISSION, ALL IS AT REST

Going a little farther, he fell facedown and prayed, "My Father, if it is possible, let this cup pass from me. Yet not as I will, but as you will." Matthew 26:39 CSB

What is it about the word "submission" that makes many of us uneasy? Perhaps it's because submitting requires yielding to another person's will or authority. It's human nature to resist submission, whether it's our spouse, parents, teachers, employer, government, or God. In the end, submission requires prioritizing others above ourselves, a concept we often find challenging, favoring our own desires instead. While we're called to submit to others in many ways, our ultimate allegiance and perfect submission must be to God.

For many, the idea of relinquishing control, and the vulnerability that comes with it, makes the concept of perfect submission feel unattainable. But what if we could perfectly submit to God's will in every aspect of life? What would that look like? I imagine it would look much like Christ in the Garden of Gethsemane.

On the eve of his crucifixion, Jesus, overcome with anguish, fell face down in the garden and prayed to his Father. The torture that was soon to come filled him with a sickening dread, but the impending separation from his Father was infinitely more terrifying, causing beads of blood to drop from his forehead. The heartfelt words of his prayer would resonate through the ages, shaping countless Christian prayers, but none ever matching the raw emotion and spiritual weight of his own: *"My Father, if it is possible, let this cup pass from me. Yet not as I will, but as you will."* This is perfect submission.

Even in perfect submission to the Father, Christ's human heart ached and rejoiced, experiencing the depth of human emotion. According to the writer of Hebrews, Jesus, in fervent prayer that evening, pleaded with loud crying and tears to God, who could save him from death.[1] This is despite the fact that the option to exercise his will was always available to him. But Christ, with unwavering resolve, embraces the cross for our sake, submitting to his Father's will.

The powerful image of Jesus repeating this prayer three times is a testament to the importance of persevering in prayer, especially when facing challenging situations. In Matthew, Mark, and Luke's gospel accounts, the final prayer is followed by a palpable sense of quiet determination. It seems that Jesus was at peace with God's decision, and his obedience would be evident in his action to go to the cross. And yes, the reality of his submission meant his subjection to the sinful control and power of humanity. But Jesus clearly told Pilate that God was in charge and that Pilate only had the power God gave him.[2]

Only through the empowering presence of the Holy Spirit can we, as believers, find the strength to humbly submit to God's will even when the outcome is not what we want. This type of

---

1. Hebrews 5:7–8

2. John 19:11

submission is beyond human capability, but thankfully, we are not alone. While the Spirit's quiet work transforms our hearts and consciences, Christ's powerful intercession with the Father on our behalf strengthens our ability to submit. Then we, like Christ, can discover that inner peace, that quiet resolve Fanny Crosby beautifully terms "rest."

Saturday, Day 28

REFLECTION DAY

Listen to your favorite version of "Blessed Assurance" while reading the lyrics.

Among all the lines in the hymn, which one resonates with you the most? It could be one from this week's devotional or a new one. Write it in the space below.

Think about a relevant Bible passage that corresponds to this line, and write it in the space provided.

Explain your reasoning for connecting the Bible passage with the line you provided.

Monday, Day 29

"HOW GREAT THOU ART"—A HISTORY

T he unexpected deluge of meeting requests had kept Bev in New York all summer despite his original plans. But that was just fine with him, he thought, as a slow smile stretched across his face. He was enjoying every minute. Now, just as he had done nearly every night for sixteen long weeks, he rose to the occasion as the music began and a familiar rush of adrenaline coursed through him. Gripping the microphone at the lectern for the hundredth time, his voice boomed with the familiar opening lines of "O Lord my God, when I in awesome wonder...." Visibly moved by the soaring melody, the crowd sang along, their voices a wave of emotion washing over the performer.

It was George Beverly Shea's unmistakable voice that filled the lectern each night as he sang at the 1957 Billy Graham Crusades at Madison Square Garden. This unprecedented sixteen-week event drew over 2.3 million people and resulted in over 61,000 professions of faith. That summer also launched what has been ranked by *Christianity Today* as the second most popular hymn, behind "Amazing Grace." However, the version we sing today, while sharing a common ancestor with a Swedish poem, has evolved significantly in melody and lyrics.

Its original author, Carl Boberg, was born on August 16, 1859, in the small, quiet town of Monsteras, in southeastern Sweden, to a carpenter and his wife. A short stint as a sailor and many other professions filled his restless youth. But at nineteen, Boberg found his calling, giving his life to Christ and attending Bible college. He later returned to his hometown and preached at the Mission Covenant Church. There, he also found success as an author and editor of the town's newspaper. Later in life, he would be elected to the Swedish Parliament and deemed a radical because of his opinions on drinking, pacifism, and the church. However, it was what would happen one summer day when he was just twenty-six that would forever etch his name in history.

Boberg, in his own words, explained the day this way: "It was in 1885, and in the time of year when everything seemed to be in its richest coloring; the birds were singing in trees and wherever they could find a perch. On a particular afternoon, some friends and I had been to Kronobäck where we had participated in an afternoon service. As we were returning, a thunderstorm began to appear on the horizon. We hurried to shelter. There were loud claps of thunder, and the lighting flashed across the sky. Strong winds swept over the meadows and billowing fields of grain. However, the storm was soon over and the clear sky appeared with a beautiful rainbow. When I arrived home, the lake across from my home reflected like a mirror in the sky above, and a church bell rung out in the distance. It was then that I fell to my knees in humble praise to the God who holds all of creation in his hands. That same evening, I wrote a poem which I titled, 'O Store Gud.'"

An earlier literal English translation of four of Boberg's stanzas began, "O mighty God, when I behold the wonder, Of nature's beauty, wrought by words of Thine, And how Thou leadest all from realms up yonder, Sustaining earthly life in love benign."

Boberg had no plans to set the poem to music but published it in the Monsteras *Times* the following spring, in 1886. Afterward, the poem was largely forgotten and appeared headed for obscurity. What Boberg didn't know was that some unknown Swede had read his poem in the newspaper, had set it to a popular folk tune, and was singing it in his church. The congregation loved the uplifting words and melody and quickly shared it with other churches in the surrounding provinces. Some years later, while attending a church conference, Boberg was amazed to hear his poem being used in congregational hymn singing. Seeing how well received it was, he republished it in 1891 in the newspaper he now was currently editing, complete with the musical score.

In the following two decades, Boberg's Swedish hymn saw its simple yet powerful words translated into German, Polish, and Russian, undergoing slight alterations to better resonate with each new audience. However, the hymn's slow rise to fame would not begin until a Ukrainian church would sing the Russian version for British missionaries Reverend Stuart K. Hine and his wife, Mercy.

In 1931 thirty-two-year-old Stuart Wesley Keene Hine, a missionary in the Carpathian Mountains of Ukraine, first heard the Russian translation from the German text of the hymn. The song became a favorite of both Hine and his wife, who used it in their evangelistic work. Over the next fifteen to twenty years, the young missionary refined the hymn, adding verses inspired by his personal experiences and unique spiritual journey. The first three stanzas were written during his time in the Carpathian Mountains. But the outbreak of war in 1939 forced Hine and his wife to flee Russia and make the difficult return to a war-torn England. There, they would use the hymn with Polish refugees, adding the fourth stanza after the war.

In 1949 Hine finished his English translation and published it that same year alongside the Russian version in his gospel magazine, *Grace and Peace*. The magazine had a wide circulation among refugees in fifteen countries around the world. In addition, British missionaries spread the English version to former British colonies in Africa and India.

It was at a small village near Deolali, India, where traveling theologian and evangelist J. Edwin Orr heard the hymn being sung by a choir of the Naga tribe. He was so moved by the song's message and melody that he eagerly showcased it at the Forest Home Christian Conference Center in the San Bernardino Mountains of Southern California.

Around the same time, Tim Spencer, a former singing cowboy who'd shared the stage with Roy Rogers, launched Manna Music, a publishing company based in Burbank, California. Spencer's children, Hal and Loretta, were in attendance at Orr's conference and brought the hymn's sheet music home to their father. Spencer quickly negotiated with Hine to purchase the rights of the song, making minor adjustments before publishing it.

Eventually the song found its way into the hands of George Beverly Shea, the famed soloist, and Cliff Barrows, longtime music and program director for the Billy Graham Evangelistic Association. They collaborated closely with Hine to get the song ready for their crusades. While it was performed at the Toronto crusade in 1955, the song's breakout success came with its performance at the Madison Square Garden crusade in 1957.

Shea, capitalizing on Billy Graham's massive audience, brought the song to a national audience through live radio performances, stadium concerts before thousands, and televised events like the sixteen-week crusade at Madison Square Garden, which attracted an estimated ninety-six million total viewers. And the adoption of "How Great Thou Art" as the theme song for Billy Graham's weekly radio program in 1959 brought the hymn to widespread national attention.

Within ten years, the hymn had been translated into over a dozen languages and sung worldwide. The song boasts a staggering 1,800 recorded versions across seventy-five years, with Elvis Presley's powerful renditions consistently setting the standard for all others. Elvis won four Grammy Awards in his lifetime; two were for his recordings of the hymn—one a 1967 studio version and the other a 1974 live performance.

On that stormy summer day in 1885, with strong winds and heavy rain pelting Boberg's face, he probably wasn't pleased about being caught in such a dangerous storm. However, the storm and its aftermath left an indelible mark on him, revealing the awesomeness of God. Thankfully, he recorded his observations, which would later be revised and become a testimony to the greatness of God for countless generations across the globe.

Lyrics Disclaimer

Due to copyright restrictions and the associated licensing costs, the entire lyrics of "How Great Thou Art" have been excluded from this book. However, the lyrics are readily available online.

Tuesday, Day 30

O LORD MY GOD, WHEN I IN AWESOME WONDER, CONSIDER ALL THE WORKS THY HANDS HAVE MADE

The heavens declare the glory of God, and the sky displays what his hands have made. Psalm 19:1 GWT

King David didn't need a scientific explanation for God's existence. The world was his classroom, and for him, nature's lessons were easy to understand. Although David could have described other wonders of God's creation, his focus in this psalm was on the splendor of the heavens—and perhaps for good reason. Many people will never see majestic mountain peaks, boundless oceans, or awe-inspiring canyons let alone the Seven Wonders of the World, yet the sky is accessible to everyone everywhere.

David's celestial observations were made without complicated calculations or high-powered telescopes. His knowledge was probably honed over years spent as a shepherd, with the starlit sky as his only teacher. As he gazed up at the night sky, the varied colors of the horizon seemed to him like the handiwork of a skilled craftsman. And with the breathtaking panorama of the stars, moon, and lingering sunset, he felt certain of an intelligent Creator who was worthy of worship.

David's use of the present tense with the words "declares" and "displays" emphasizes the continuous revelation of God's glory. He saw nature as a living testament to God's creative genius, an ongoing, tangible expression of his divine power and wisdom that was constantly unveiling new facets of his being. Even now, as our comprehension of the universe expands, its breathtaking complexity affirms a purposeful design by God.

The Apostle Paul conveyed a similar message, asserting that nature, from the dawn of creation, has clearly displayed God's infinite wisdom, immense power, and timeless existence.[1] This revelation of God in nature is accessible to all, leaving no one without understanding or excuse.

Even Albert Einstein, to his dismay, found the intricate design of the universe compelling evidence for a divine hand and higher intelligence. Though Einstein was an unbeliever, he declared that the wonders of the universe "reveal an intelligence of such superiority that, compared with it, all the systematic thinking and acting of human beings is an utterly insignificant reflection."

We must avoid, however, conflating nature with the full revelation of God's character as found in the Scriptures and embodied by Jesus Christ. It's important to appreciate, though, that nature does communicate with us in a way Scripture does not. We can learn so much about God by studying his creation. As you gaze upon the vast expanse of stars, remember that he placed each and every one of them in place, their shimmering

---

1. Romans 1:20

light set to twinkle just for you. Through the magnificence of the skies—a celestial tapestry of the stars, moon, sun, and planets—we get a glimpse of the awe-inspiring character of God.

Wednesday, Day 31

THEN SINGS MY SOUL, MY SAVIOR GOD, TO THEE; HOW GREAT THOU ART, HOW GREAT THOU ART!

Praise the Lord, O my soul. And all that is within me, praise His holy name. Psalm 103:1 NLV

Roman prisons were filthy, dark, underground dungeons with little to no ventilation. Instead of individual cells, groups of prisoners were chained together in overcrowded rooms and subjected to psychological and physical torture designed to extract confessions. Paul and Silas found themselves in a prison not unlike this one, and they faced a tough decision: Would they succumb to the relentless psychological torment, or would they find strength in their faith, praising God in their circumstances?[1]

---

1. Acts 16:16–40

If anyone had reason to be bitter and angry and to complain about their circumstances, they did. Their act of freeing a female slave from a demonic spirit's grasp was what had landed them in prison. Her owners realized they could no longer profit from the girl and had Paul and Silas stripped, mercilessly beaten with rods, and cast into the darkest corner of the prison, where their feet were secured in stocks. Wouldn't anyone feel bitter and angry in that situation? If they were doing God's work, shouldn't he have protected them?

As heavy chains bit into their flesh, Paul and Silas lay in the oppressive darkness, their bodies wracked with pain, their limbs stiff and immobile. The other prisoners, their faces etched with despair, shared their same burden, each wondering what tomorrow held, believing a swift death preferable to their current torment. Then, suddenly, out of the darkness, arose singing that seemed to silence the mournful cries of the other prisoners.

The heartfelt singing of hymns and praise to God suddenly began to reverberate through the prison walls, comforting the other prisoners. While the exact hymns sung are unknown, the image of Paul and Silas, their bodies bruised and battered, powerfully singing Psalm 119 as their voices ring through the stone prison walls, seems possible. Whether those outside the prison could hear, we know God did, and he answered with a powerful earthquake that shook the very foundation of the prison, throwing open the heavy doors and rattling the chains from every prisoner's limbs.

God had a plan far grander than anything Paul or Silas could have imagined. Their simple act of praying and worshipping God through their own pain brought comfort to their fellow prisoners, evident from the fact that none escaped when given the chance. Paul and Silas also never could have seen the salvation of the worried jailer and his entire family. And Paul's public shaming of the magistrate—demanding his and Silas's release after their unlawful beating since they were Roman citizens—would hopefully imply the need for more careful treatment of Christians in the future.

The verse's phrase, "all that is within me," speaks to a whole-life praise of God, encompassing both triumphs and struggles. God deserves all the praise and adoration that a person's entire being can possibly give. The concept is simple enough to grasp, but applying it during life's tougher times is a real challenge. Examine every aspect of your soul this Lent to see if you're giving God the full praise he deserves. Only then, as you pour out your soul in praise, will you grasp the boundless nature of God's greatness.

AND WHEN I THINK, THAT GOD, HIS SON NOT SPARING, SENT HIM TO DIE, I SCARCE CAN TAKE IT IN

He did not even spare his own Son but gave him up for us all. How will he not also with him grant us everything? Romans 8:32 CSB

Guilt is a powerful motivator. Despite God's forgiveness, many Christians still wrestle with guilt over past sins, unable to forgive themselves. They recall Scripture about God removing our sins from us as far as the east is from the west and casting them into the depths of the sea or even that he remembers them no more.[1] Nevertheless, the impact of past bad choices can be significant, leaving one to contend with lasting consequences and emotional turmoil. Even though God washes

---

1. Micah 7:19, Psalm 103:12, Hebrews 8:12

away our sins, the effects of sin can persist, a daily reminder of our past mistakes.

This dilemma was something Paul understood better than most. As a zealous Pharisee, he relentlessly hunted down Christians before his conversion, leading to their imprisonment and, frequently, their deaths. The weight of his past actions hung heavily on his conscience with the crushing burden of guilt and regret. His past clung to him, and those he sought to minister to early on remembered it too and were justifiably wary. He suffered not only from the internal guilt but also from the external judgment of others.

This might explain why Paul dedicates the entirety of Romans 8 to arguing that Jesus' sacrifice on the cross guarantees our freedom from sin and guilt. The manifestation of this guarantee is the Holy Spirit's power working in our lives. As believers, the Spirit helps us cast off the heavy burden of our sinful, guilty thoughts, choosing instead the life-giving guidance of the Spirit.

While the aforementioned passages on forgiveness are helpful, Paul urged a fresh perspective, a shift in our understanding of what it means to be forgiven. His argument was clear and straightforward: God didn't spare his own sinless Son but allowed him to be brutally killed and nailed to a shameful cross for all of us. Given this, why hesitate to believe he'll also generously give us everything else we need?

The finality and ultimate outcome of Jesus' death on the cross means that no one can bring any additional guilty charge against those whom God has redeemed. God, who is the highest judge, has already declared a believer not guilty and right with him. Who, then, can say they are still guilty? No one!

It is time to forgive yourself for past mistakes and let go of any guilt. Instead, let them serve as reminders that you are a new creation, free from the desires of your old life. The profound truth is that God is for us and is working out his ultimate purpose for our lives, which is to make us more like Christ. Remember that God's immeasurable love for you led him to sacrifice his own Son, Jesus, to pay the price for your sins. Now, believer, let yourself be fully convinced! How could he not also set you free from everything else?

Friday, Day 33

WHEN CHRIST SHALL COME, WITH SHOUT OF ACCLAMATION; AND TAKE ME HOME, WHAT JOY SHALL FILL MY HEART!

For the Lord himself will descend from heaven with a shout, with the archangel's voice, and with the trumpet of God, and the dead in Christ will rise first. Then we who are still alive, who are left, will be caught up together with them in the clouds to meet the Lord in the air, and so we will always be with the Lord. 1 Thessalonians 4:16–17 CSB

Stuart Hine was captivated by Carl Boberg's hymn from the very first time he heard it. For years, he and his wife sang the Russian version on the Ukrainian mission field, sharing it with the locals. In the small villages where he would preach, Hine recognized that his parishioners, though loving God, didn't fully grasp the extent of God's love for them. He felt strongly that the greatness of God's love was a message that needed to be shared, particularly in the impoverished villages they ministered to, and the hymn became a powerful tool in that mission.

The more he shared how great God was, the more it influenced the composition of a new yet similar hymn. While translating Boberg's original hymn into English, Hine added new verses, resulting in the version we sing today. His journey across the Carpathian Mountains inspired the first three verses, while the fourth was composed nearly a decade later.

In 1939 World War II exploded across Europe, forcing Hine to return to England. During the war, he continued his evangelistic work at home, using the first three verses of his new hymn whenever possible. In the war's aftermath, the Hines were surprised to find England overwhelmed by millions of Eastern European refugees yearning to go home. In 1948 he visited one such Russian refugee camp in Sussex, England. Inspired by one of the refugees' testimony and his longing for Christ to return, Hine wrote the hymn's fourth verse.

According to the story, the man had been separated from his wife at the end of the war and had not seen her since. When they separated, she was a Christian, but he wasn't but since had become one. He longed to be with her so they could finally share their faith together. Sadly, though, he accepted the fact that they might never meet in this life again but held onto hope for their eternal reunion in heaven. Hine found inspiration in the man's hopeful words and shaped his final verse around them.

Hine's final verse depicts a future where the call of Jesus Christ summons all Christians, living and dead, to their eternal home with him. In that moment, our hearts will overflow with a joy so profound, so complete, that no earthly experience could compare.

Saturday, Day 34
REFLECTION DAY

Listen to your favorite version of "How Great Thou Art" while reading the lyrics.

Among all the lines in the hymn, which one resonates with you the most? It could be one from this week's devotional or a new one. Write it in the space below.

Think about a relevant Bible passage that corresponds to this line, and write it in the space provided.

Explain your reasoning for connecting the Bible passage with the line you provided.

"AMAZING GRACE"—A HISTORY

"Amazing Grace" is arguably one of the most popular, widely recorded, and recognizable songs in the English-speaking world. Its enduring message of forgiveness and grace available to everyone regardless of their past has resonated with millions over the last two hundred fifty years. But the lyrics also tell another incredible story of a wicked slave trader who, at best, deserved death at sea but survived countless dangers, diseases, abuse, and near-death experiences only to find redemption and God's amazing grace.

In 1725 John Newton was born in Wapping, a London riverside district bustling with maritime trade. His father was a merchant ship captain who was frequently away at sea on voyages lasting two or three years. His mother was a devout Christian who taught their only child to read the Bible and attend church regularly. Though she hoped her son would one day become a preacher, she died from tuberculosis when he was just six years old. With his father at sea, the young boy was temporarily entrusted to the care of his mother's close friends, the Catlett family, who lived in Kent.

As a child, Newton would spend the next several years at a boarding school, where he was severely mistreated. He hoped life would get better with his father and his new wife in Essex, but it didn't. Sadly, his father's long absences left him with an emotionally distant stepmother who made life difficult for him.

When he was just eleven, his father brought him along on his ship as an apprentice, where he would make six long voyages before turning seventeen. The rough-and-tumble world of sailors presented a moral challenge for Newton, forcing him to choose between his mother's Christian influence and the sea's carefree existence. He ultimately chose the latter, leaving his childhood beliefs behind. When his father retired from seafaring in 1742, he arranged for his son to work at a sugarcane plantation in Jamaica. Newton, however, had other ideas and joined another merchant ship sailing out to the Mediterranean Sea.

Over the years, he maintained a close relationship with the Catlett family, mainly because of their daughter, Mary, whom he would later marry. Through all of life's challenges, Newton always aimed to return to her, no matter what happened. While traveling to visit her in 1743, he was captured and forced into service in the British Navy, enduring five harsh and turbulent years abroad.

Serving as a midshipman, the lowest-ranking officer, aboard *HMS Harwich*, he quickly gained a reputation for insubordination, debauchery, and shocking profanity, proving ill-suited to naval life. Following a botched escape, he was punished with eight dozen lashes and demoted to an ordinary seaman. He even tried to murder the captain and commit suicide.

Wishing to be free of Newton, the captain traded him into service on a slave ship sailing for West Africa. However, his failure to get along with the new crew and his open mocking of the captain resulted in his imprisonment and being chained like the slaves they carried. Upon reaching Sierra Leone, the captain sold Newton into slavery to a local trader, whose wife, an African princess, subjected Newton and her other slaves to harsh treatment. After more than a year of such treatment and believing he would never leave, he managed to get a letter to his father describing his circumstances. His father successfully rescued his son in 1748, sending a ship's captain aboard the *Greyhound* with orders to return him home safely.

On the return voyage to England, Newton was given a copy of *The Christian's Pattern*, also known as *The Imitation of Christ*, by Thomas à Kempis. The fifteenth century devotional highlights the significance of nurturing a profound prayer life. In a matter of weeks, Newton would put what he was reading into practice when a violent storm threatened to capsize their ship.

For days on end, the crew battled against the relentless waves as they struggled to keep the ship afloat. On one occasion, as Newton was about to leave the deck, a rogue wave crashed over the side, sweeping the crewman who had replaced him into the churning sea. To prevent being washed overboard himself, Newton and a shipmate secured themselves to the ship's pump and worked for hours bailing out the ship.

Prior to this storm, Newton considered himself an atheist. Not only had he disregarded the faith his mother had diligently instilled in him but he actively opposed it, mocking believers and condemning God as a myth. But battered by the storm's fury and struggling against the elements, he found himself reflecting on his past mistakes, heightening his sense of regret. He believed only divine intervention could save them and in desperation cried out to God, promising that if he lived, he would serve him for the rest of his days.

When the tattered remains of the ship finally landed on the Irish coast about two weeks later, Newton made his way to the nearest church, his heart filled with a profound sense of gratitude and relief. He later wrote of his growing conviction that God had sent him a powerful message in that storm and at that moment began a work in him.

Although Newton's conversion to Christianity wasn't immediate, the seeds of faith had been sown, gradually changing his perspective over time. Safely home, he immediately wrote to the Catlett family to ask for Mary's hand in marriage. He couldn't offer her financial security, but her positive response spurred him to seek his fortune, this time by working aboard a slave ship bound for Charleston, South Carolina.

For the next six years, Newton remained involved in the slave trade, eventually captaining his own ships that acquired slaves from major ports and transported them to America. Unlike before, he now encouraged prayer among his sailors and insisted on humane treatment of their human cargo. Nevertheless, Newton's public condemnation of the slave trade did not occur for another forty years.

His 1750 marriage to Mary prompted him to seriously consider abandoning seafaring life as he found their separations increasingly difficult. His future was decided for him in 1755 when he suffered a devastating stroke at the age of thirty, leaving him unable to return to sea. He later reflected on his health problems, which, while unwelcomed at the time, provided the break he needed from a life he felt trapped in. This was, for him, a step forward in his spiritual development.

Newton and his wife moved to Liverpool in 1756, where he began working as a customs agent. Once settled in, his interest in Christianity was ignited. He taught himself Latin, Greek, and theology, and he and Mary became deeply involved in their local church. His friends were so impressed by his passion that they suggested he become a priest in the Church of England. But ordination was not possible for Newton through typical means because of his lack of a university education.

Instead, Newton started writing about his tumultuous past with vivid descriptions of his experiences, instantly grabbing the attention of clergymen John Fawcett and Thomas Haweis. In

1764 the two men persuaded Newton to painstakingly detail his life's journey in a series of letters, eventually brought together and published as *An Authentic Narrative of Some Remarkable Particulars in the Life of Reverend John Newton*. Inspired by Newton's life, British statesman Lord Dartmouth recommended him for a church position. In 1764 he was ordained in the Church of England and became the curate of Olney, Buckinghamshire.

Unlike other clergymen of his time, Newton openly shared his personal stories, experiences, and struggles with sin in his sermons. This made him relatable to his congregation, a group that included the poet William Cowper. Encouraged by his newfound friendship with Cowper and the prevailing notion that clergymen should also be poets, Newton began writing hymns to enhance his weekly sermons.

In his 1773 New Year's Day sermon based on 1 Chronicles 17:16–17, Newton recounted his own profound conversion experience during that fateful storm—an experience that "saved a wretch like me." The sermon was titled "Faith's Review and Expectation," and his corresponding hymn began with the words "Amazing grace." Whether the six stanzas he wrote were sung to music or chanted by the congregation remains unclear, but it was on this day that Newton and his congregation first sang "Amazing Grace."

At first the hymn served merely as a supplement to a sermon, and it's possible he never intended it to be anything more. However, in 1779 he and Cowper bound and published the hymn anonymously under the title *Olney Hymns*, for which Newton contributed 280 of the 348 texts.

The hymn might have faded into obscurity in England over the next fifty years, but American composer William Walker rediscovered it during the Second Great Awakening, a Protestant religious revival that swept across the United States. In 1835 Walker set it to the tune "New Britain," the melody we sing today, and published it in his bestselling songbook, *The Southern Harmony and Musical Companion*.

Interestingly, Harriet Beecher Stowe, in her impactful 1852 anti-slavery novel, *Uncle Tom's Cabin*, contributed a new verse to "Amazing Grace," as sung by Tom. This new verse had been passed down orally in African American communities for at least fifty years and opened with the lines, *When we've been there ten thousand years, Bright shining as the sun, We've no less days to sing God's praise, Than when we first begun.*

It would take another fifty years before the evangelical composer Edwin Othello Excell would publish the hymn as we know it today. He streamlined Newton's hymn by reducing the original six stanzas to three and added the final verse from *Uncle Tom's Cabin*. The fifth and sixth stanzas of Newton's original work are rarely heard in American churches today.

Today "Amazing Grace" is performed an estimated ten million times a year and appears on over 11,000 albums. Across cultures and generations, the hymn's moving message of forgiveness and spiritual healing through God's grace has touched countless hearts, securing its place as the most beloved hymn in history.

"Amazing Grace" has no direct connection to the British abolition of slavery. However, in 1780 Newton left behind the quiet countryside of Olney to assume his new post as rector of St. Mary Woolnoth in London. It was there he met a young William Wilberforce, who was attending his church. Serving as Wilberforce's mentor, Newton would later guide the young lawmaker through his parliamentary campaign to abolish the slave trade. This campaign culminated in the 1806 ban and the liberation of over 800,000 enslaved people. Newton passed away the following year at the age of eighty-two.

Considering John Newton's early life, it's tempting to conclude he was unworthy of God's grace. His wickedness and profanity were matched only by his ruthless exploitation of others through enslavement and brutality. Judging by his auto-biography, Newton would likely concur; he considered himself a failure in almost every aspect of his life. Near the end of his life, weakened by illness and a failing memory, he declared, "My memory is nearly gone, but I remember two things: that I am a great sinner and that Christ is a great Savior!"

Even though our life experiences may not mirror that of Newton, none of us is deserving of God's amazing grace. However, the joy and peace of escaping physical and spiritual destruction are something we can all understand as we all share the human experience of sin. This is why the universal appeal of the hymn's message of God's saving grace, embracing even the most sinful, has endured for over two hundred fifty years, touching hearts with its powerful message of forgiveness and second chances.

"Amazing Grace" Lyrics

Amazing grace! How sweet the sound
That saved a wretch like me!
I once was lost, but now am found;
Was blind, but now I see.

Through many dangers, toils and snares,
I have already come;
Tis grace hath brought me safe thus far,
And grace will lead me home.

The Lord has promised good to me,
His Word my hope secures;
He will my Shield and Portion be,
As long as life endures.

Yea, when this flesh and heart shall fail,
And mortal life shall cease,
I shall possess, within the veil,
A life of joy and peace.

The earth shall soon dissolve like snow,
The sun forbear to shine;
But God, who called me here below,
Will be forever mine.

When we've been there ten thousand years,
Bright shining as the sun,
We've no less days to sing God's praise
Than when we'd first begun.

Tuesday, Day 36

AMAZING GRACE, HOW SWEET THE SOUND THAT SAVED A WRETCH LIKE ME

But God, who is rich in mercy, because of his great love that he had for us, made us alive with Christ even though we were dead in trespasses. You are saved by grace! Ephesians 2:4–5 CSB

Is the sound of amazing grace still sweet to you? I'm not referring to the hymn's melody or lyrics but to the overwhelming, intangible presence of God's grace. Although living the Christian life is a blessing, we must actively guard against the insidious growth of callousness to our past sins—in other words, forgetting the "wretch" we were before coming to Christ. Otherwise, we risk becoming self-righteous judges, blinded by our own perceived righteousness and forgetting our own past failings and the undeserved grace that transformed us. Worse yet, we risk growing numb to the ever-present sting of sin in our own lives.

When John Newton composed "Amazing Grace" during the 1773 Christmas season, he had been a believer for at least twenty years. But for Newton, traces of his past sinful life remained—or at least the memory of the "wretch" he was. Unlike most of us, who would prefer to bury past transgressions, Newton was driven to share his with others. His motivation stemmed not from pride but from humility as he considered it a wonderful opportunity to demonstrate the magnificent power of God's grace.

Newton refused to let the weight of his past mistakes hold him back, choosing instead to focus on the present. The consequences of his actions remained, but the incredible reality of God's grace filled him with a sense of peace and overwhelming joy, washing away the pain. His reflection on the past served only to highlight God's incredible grace in saving him. His own words painted a picture of his utter unworthiness, yet God saved him anyway.

What makes grace so amazing after all? To begin with, it saves you from spiritual death and eternal separation from God! Consider this: At any moment before your conversion, death could have claimed you while you were still in your sins. Yet God, in his boundless love, actively sought you out, offering rescue even though you were his enemy, undeserving of such kindness or grace. I would call that amazing! It's a shame that today the core message of salvation seems to have been sanitized to erase the horror of what awaits those that do not believe.

But there's something else about grace that's amazing: its capacity for transformation in this life. According to the Apostle Paul, the Christian is made alive in Christ to fulfill God's purpose here on Earth. Sealed by the Holy Spirit, we enjoy a direct relationship with God, unshackling us from the weight of past sins and strengthening us to face life's struggles. With a renewed perspective, we find peace, joy, and a deep love for all those around us. That's amazing too!

Perhaps what is most amazing about God's grace is what it cost for him to give us that grace. His love for us was so great that he sacrificed his one and only Son on a cruel cross to pay the price for our sins. His gift of grace is unbelievably good—amazing because we don't deserve it—and yet it's been given to us, wretched as we are.

Wednesday, Day 37

I WAS LOST, BUT NOW I'M FOUND. WAS BLIND, BUT NOW I SEE

He answered, "Whether or not he's a sinner, I don't know. One thing I do know: I was blind, and now I can see!" John 9:25 CSB

What fascinates me most about this account of Jesus healing the man born blind isn't the miracle itself—though it was undeniably wonderful. The Gospels frequently mention Jesus' miracles, most commonly his healing of the blind. I'm most struck by the man's courage in confronting the Pharisees after the healing. The truth is, John spends more time on this story element than he does on the healing itself.

What do we actually know about this man? To begin with, he was blind and likely taken by his parents to a begging spot each day. Not only that but he lived with the social stigma that either his sins or his parents' sins had somehow triggered his blindness. And unlike other boys, he probably didn't have a standard Jewish education, which involved learning to read, write, and memorize significant portions of the Torah, starting around age five or six. Then, beginning around age ten or eleven, studies included oral interpretations of the Torah as well as developing skills in questioning and debating. Following Bar Mitzvah at age twelve, boys commonly pursued a trade or went into business. It's unlikely he received any of that, as disabled people were often viewed as a drain on family and community resources.

We can only imagine how much better his life would be now that he could see. He could now work, raise a family, attend synagogue, and be an active member of his community. Before, his disability would have greatly limited him, and society had already condemned him for his blindness. His entire life had been spent lonely, in utter darkness, having visually witnessed none of God's creation—no light, sky, structures, or people. It's safe to say that his life was about to improve dramatically!

Setting aside his physical healing, it still doesn't explain how he managed to outwit some of the foremost scholars of his time. It makes sense that suddenly being able to see would now give him a new understanding of the visual world around him. However, there was another aspect to his healing process that no medicine could produce.

It was like a light had been switched on inside him, and not only could he see the physical world but the spiritual one as well. Somehow, in his healing, he had simultaneously received a profound spiritual awareness he'd never known before. Now, with the confidence of a spiritual giant, he could boldly debate the mysteries of God, engaging in spirited arguments with the most learned men in his community.

He embodied the ideal Christian because his transformation was clear to all who knew him. He testified to others of the greatness of Jesus and remained loyal to his healer despite any persecution he would face. And he also knew it was not about him, as he was content to let Jesus have all the recognition; his name remains unknown.

Like then, many today frantically search for remedies to physical disabilities as they clutch at any hope of escape from the crushing weight of their suffering. They look forward to a new life, one where renewed health and vitality bring strength and energy back into their lives. Then there are countless others that silently endure daily spiritual struggles, with the world pressing down so hard that it often mirrors the effects of physical pain. They yearn for inner peace and healing.

The fact is, we should be grateful for both physical and spiritual healings as they both hold promises of a better life. But we must also keep them in perspective as one provides temporary physical relief in this world while the other offers a lasting peace and joy that resonates within our souls for eternity.

Thursday, Day 38

THROUGH MANY DANGERS, TOILS, AND SNARES WE HAVE ALREADY COME

The Lord isn't slow to do what he promised, as some people think. Rather, he is patient for your sake. He doesn't want to destroy anyone but wants all people to have an opportunity to turn to him and change the way they think and act. 2 Peter 3:9 GWT

When singing the third verse of "Amazing Grace," we likely think of "dangers, toils, and snares" as representing the various struggles Christians face, such as suffering, temptation, persecution, and spiritual attacks, as well as the inner battles caused by our sinful nature. That is one interpretation, but I'm not sure it aligns with John Newton's original intention based on his life story, not to mention the sermon he wrote the hymn for. It's more likely that Newton was thinking about the enduring grace of God that had protected him during his troubled youth, a time when he certainly did not deserve it.

Indeed, Newton's life was marked by constant dangers and struggles, making him realize later in life just how fortunate he was to have narrowly survived each time. For instance, he was once thrown from a horse and narrowly avoided being impaled on sharp stakes. At another time, he was late to board a ship and watched from shore as it capsized, drowning all passengers aboard. While on a hunting trip in Africa, he and his companions got lost in a swamp and thought they were going to die, but an unusually bright moon led them to safety. Additionally, he managed to survive malaria, live through being enslaved, and endure being whipped eight dozen times, and he nearly drowned at sea and was shipwrecked on multiple occasions. Newton's life was filled with frequent brushes with death.

So for Newton, this verse was a practical expression of his life experiences before coming to Christ. Throughout his life, he somehow managed to survive countless near-death experiences. His explanation for his survival can be found in the next line, where he claims grace has kept him safe thus far and will one day lead him home.

What about you? How patient was God was with you before you came to know Christ? Can you think back on any close calls that still leave you wondering how you escaped unscathed? Even if your life has not been as adventurous and dangerous as Newton's, this verse is still relevant to you. In reality, there are numerous dangers that God has shielded us from without our knowledge.

God's patience with us is a truth that we should be deeply grateful for. Peter elaborates on the concept of patience in relation to God's promise of Christ's future return. He argues that any delay we notice is because of God being patient, allowing us enough time to repent. Taking into account this reality, I dare to suggest that a lot of Christians today are glad that Jesus didn't come back a decade ago, five years ago, or even two months ago. There is a compassionate purpose in God's timing. Every breath we take is a moment to be grateful for God's patience with us and to reflect on the grace that has protected us until now, knowing that this same grace will eventually lead us back home.

Friday, Day 39

WHEN WE'VE BEEN THERE TEN THOUSAND YEARS, BRIGHT SHINING AS THE SUN

Dear friends, don't ignore this fact: One day with the Lord is like a thousand years, and a thousand years are like one day. 2 Peter 3:8 GWT

Solomon tells us that life is fleeting, like a passing mist.[1] The older I get, the more this verse resonates as each passing year feels shorter than the last, like a speeding train. That, of course, isn't true. Time remains constant, but the shrinking runway of my life gives the illusion of accelerating speed, a feeling of urgency. The relentless march of time inevitably leads us to contemplate our mortality, prompting soul-searching questions about our purpose and whether we've lived a life worthy of our beliefs. And if we're honest with ourselves, whether we've checked everything off our own list.

---

1. Ecclesiastes 1:2

As the passage of time unfolds, like a play on the stage of life, with each act bringing its own set of emotions and experiences, we find ourselves wondering where it all went as we leave behind a trail of memories. According to Scripture, there's a designated time for every event under the heavens, such as being born and dying, weeping and laughing, being silent and speaking, mourning and dancing, and countless others.[2] And unlike money, which can be earned again, time is the most precious resource we have because it's finite. Once spent, it can never be recovered, making it even more crucial that we use the time given to us wisely.

This is why the concept of eternity is so hard for us to understand. Our very existence is bound by the constraints of time. God, though, isn't bound by anything and doesn't experience time in the same way as humans do, for "with the Lord a day is like a thousand years, and a thousand years are like a day." Simply put, to God, time is so vast that a day and a thousand years mean nothing.

Pause for a moment, and wrap your head around that concept. What if there was no past, present, or future ruling over you? What if you could fully enjoy each moment without the weight of past regrets or future uncertainties? If you're having a hard time imagining heaven and eternity, it's because the sheer magnificence and endless wonder of it surpasses human understanding. Paul compares our ability to comprehend such matters to looking at a blurry reflection in a mirror. However, he assures us that one day everything will be perfectly clear, although that time of understanding lies beyond our current time.[3]

---

2. Ecclesiastes 3:1–8

3. 1 Corinthians 13:12

What is clear is that this moment in time is all we've got, and it's nothing compared to eternal life. Although God placed us in time temporarily, this is not our permanent home. Someday we will leave this world and enter the infinite expanse of eternal glory, where time is of no value. There, we will be saints shining bright like the sun, and even when the equivalent of ten thousand earth years has passed, we will have just as many days to praise God as we did when we'd first begun.

Saturday, Day 40
REFLECTION DAY

Listen to your favorite version of "Amazing Grace" while reading the lyrics.

Among all the lines in the hymn, which one resonates with you the most? It could be one from this week's devotional or a new one. Write it in the space below.

Think about a relevant Bible passage that corresponds to this line, and write it in the space provided.

Explain your reasoning for connecting the Bible passage with the line you provided.

Leave a Review

Thank you again for reading this book! I hope and pray that in some way it encouraged you (and your group) to grow closer to Christ.

If you enjoyed this book, I would appreciate your leaving an honest review for the book and study on Amazon! Your review will help others know if this devotional is right for them.

It's easy and will only take a minute. Just search for "The Hymns of Easter, Alan Vermilye" on Amazon. Click on the product in the search results, and then click on reviews.

I would also love to hear from you! Drop me a note by visiting me at www.BrownChairBooks.com and clicking on "Contact."

Thank you and God bless!

Alan

The Carols of Christmas

Daily Advent Devotions on Classic Christmas Carols

Get All Three Volumes!

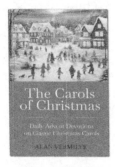

Volume 1

Carols include "O Holy Night", "I Heard the Bells on Christmas Day", "O Little Town of Bethlehem", and "Hark the Herald Angels Sing."

Volume 2

Carols include "Silent Night", "Joy to the World", "O Come All Ye Faithful", and "The First Noel".

Volume 3

Carols include "Come, Thou Long Expected Jesus", "It Came Upon the Midnight Clear", "What Child is This", and "Angels from the Realm of Glory."

www.BrownChairBooks.com

The Pilgrim's Progress Series

A Readable Modern-Day Version of the John Bunyan Classics

Get All Entire Series!

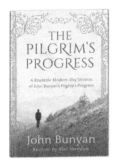

Part 1: Christian's Journey

Follow the epic adventure of Christian who leaves his home in the City of Destruction and begins a life-long quest to the Celestial City.

Part 2: Christiana's Journey

Follow the adventures of Christian's wife, Christiana, and her four boys, and a host of memorable characters who either help or hinder their progress on their journey to faith.

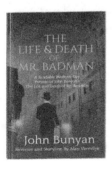

Part 3: The Life and Death of Mr. Badman

Depicts the stages of life—from cradle to grave—of a very wicked man in an evil age and the miserable consequences that undoubtedly follow such wretched living.

Study Guides Available for Each Book in the Series!

www.BrownChairBooks.com

Free Devotional

The Proverbs Devotional Challenge

31 Daily Devotions to Deepen Your Knowledge, Wisdom, and Understanding

Challenge yourself to read one chapter in Proverbs every day for 31 days straight!

The Book of Proverbs is a great source of wisdom on how to live your life according to God's desires and to gain knowledge and understanding. This book of the Bible covers topics such as life, family, parenting, friendships, work, finances, heart matters, and the power of our words.

In addition, I've created 31 devotions, one for each day, to help you explore valuable insights and apply them to your life. It's free to download as a PDF.

If you want to grow spiritually, intellectually, and emotionally, this challenge is ideal for you. The Proverbs Devotional Challenge is a great way to deepen your faith, no matter where you are on your journey.

Get Your Free Devotional Today!
www.BrownChairBooks.com/FreeDevo

The C.S. Lewis Study Series

The Most Trusted Study Guides to Learning the Works of C.S. Lewis

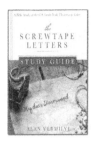

The Screwtape Letters Study Guide

A brilliant and satirical look at spiritual warfare and the dynamics of temptation.

Mere Christianity Study Guide

Become an expert on Lewis' most popular apologetics classic.

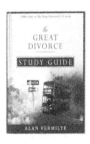

The Great Divorce Study Guide

This classic allegorical tale of heaven and hell will captivate you.

The Problem of Pain Study Guide

A philosophical approach to helping you find meaning and hope amid the pain.

The Practice of the Presence of God

A 40-Day Devotion Based on Brother Lawrence's The Practice of the Presence of God

By Alan Vermilye

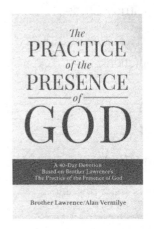

Since it was first published in 1691, The Practice of the Presence of God contains a collection of notes, letters, and interviews given by Brother Lawrence to his friends as a way of helping them turn ordinary daily life events into conversations with God.

Based on this timeless classic, The Practice of the Presence of God: A 40-Day Devotion guides readers on a 40-day journey through the wisdom of Brother Lawrence, related Scripture passages, and devotional thoughts that bring you into a more conversational relationship with God.

What others are saying:

"I love this devotional. It is short and to the point, and thus making it easy to stick to every day!" – Kathleen

"Enlightening new depths in prayer." – Kathy

"This devotional opens the door to Brother Lawrence that brings his letters and conversations to life every day!" – Steve

www.BrownChairBooks.com

It's a Wonderful Life Study Guide

A Bible Study Based on the Christmas Classic It's a Wonderful Life

By Alan Vermilye

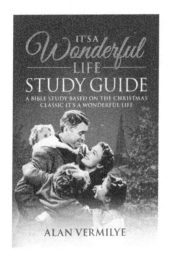

It's a Wonderful Life is one of the most popular and heart-warming films ever made. It's near-universal appeal and association with Christmas has provided a rich story of redemption that has inspired generations for decades.

It's a Wonderful Life Study Guide examines this beloved holiday classic and reminds us how easily we can become distracted from what is truly meaningful in life. This five-week Bible study experience comes complete with discussion questions for each session, Scripture references, detailed character sketches, movie summary, and related commentary. In addition, a complete answer guide and video segments for each session are available for free online.

What others are saying:

"Thank you, Alan, for the unforgettable experience. Your book has prompted me to see and learn much more than merely enjoying the film, It's a Wonderful Life." – Er Jwee

"The questions got us all thinking, and the answers provided were insightful and encouraging. I would definitely encourage Home Groups to study this!" – Jill

"It's a Wonderful Life Study Guide by Alan Vermilye is intelligent, innovative, interesting, involving, insightful, and inspirational." – Paul

www.BrownChairBooks.com

A Christmas Carol Study Guide

Book and Bible Study Based on A Christmas Carol

By Alan Vermilye

A Christmas Carol Book and Bible Study Guide includes the entire book of this Dickens classic as well as Bible study discussion questions for each chapter, Scripture references, and related commentary.

Detailed character sketches and an easy-to-read book summary provide deep insights into each character while examining the book's themes of greed, isolation, guilt, blame, compassion, generosity, transformation, forgiveness, and, finally, redemption. To help with those more difficult discussion questions, a complete answer guide is available for free online.

What others are saying:

"The study is perfect for this time of the year, turning our focus to the reason for the season—Jesus—and the gift of redemption we have through him." – Connie

"I used this for an adult Sunday School class. We all loved it!" – John

"This study is wonderful!" – Lori

"I found this a refreshing look at the Bible through the eyes of Ebenezer Scrooge's life." – Lynelle

Made in the USA
Monee, IL
08 February 2025

11761449R00079